CONTENTS

EPISCOPAL CHURCH FOUNDATION'S MISSION STATEMENT pg. i

FOREWORD pg. ii

ACKNOWLEDGMENTS pg. iii

PREFACE pg. iv

CHAPTER 1
THE MISSION-FOCUSED VESTRY pg. 1

1.1 Vestry Responsibilities .... pg. 2
1.2 Being a Vestry Member in Today's Church .... pg. 2
1.3 Focus on the Mission & Vision of the Congregation .... pg. 4
1.4 Building Leadership for Today & Tomorrow .... pg. 5
1.5 The Power of Collaboration .... pg. 6
1.6 Discussion Questions .... pg. 7
1.7 Related Resources .... pg. 7

CHAPTER 2
THE MINISTRY OF THE VESTRY: GOVERNANCE, STRUCTURE, & SELECTION pg. 8

2.1 Governance .... pg. 9
2.2 Vestry Structure .... pg. 11
2.3 Vestry Leadership .... pg. 13
2.4 Building a Healthy Vestry .... pg. 14
2.5 Discussion Questions .... pg. 16
2.6 Related Resources .... pg. 16

CHAPTER 3
BUILDING STRONG LEADERSHIP TEAMS pg. 17

3.1 A New Team Every Year .... pg. 18
3.2 Working as a Team .... pg. 21
3.3 Saying Thank You .... pg. 24
3.4 Discussion Questions .... pg. 25
3.5 Related Resources .... pg. 25

CHAPTER 4
VISION & STRATEGIC THINKING pg. 26

4.1 Discerning Mission & Vision .... pg. 27
4.2 Vision & Strategic Thinking .... pg. 29
4.3 Leading Change .... pg. 32
4.4 Discussion Questions .... pg. 34
4.5 Related Resources .... pg. 34

CHAPTER 5
FINANCE & ADMINISTRATION pg. 35

5.1 Financial Management .... pg. 36
5.2 Property Management .... pg. 41
5.3 Human Resource Management .... pg. 42
5.4 Safeguarding Our Communities ...... pg. 44
5.5 Discussion Questions .... pg. 46
5.6 Related Resources .... pg. 46

CHAPTER 6
STEWARDSHIP & VISION pg. 47

6.1 Stewardship Is More than an Annual Campaign .... pg. 48
6.2 Resources for Today & Tomorrow ..... pg. 49
6.3 Discussion Questions .... pg. 55
6.4 Related Resources .... pg. 55

CHAPTER 7
CLERGY TRANSITION pg. 56

7.1 Transition Overview .... pg. 57
7.2 Saying Goodbye .... pg. 59
7.3 Interim Lay & Clergy Leadership ...... pg. 60
7.4 The Search Process .... pg. 61
7.5 A Warm Welcome & a New Beginning ..... pg. 64
7.6 Discussion Questions .... pg. 66
7.7 Related Resources .... pg. 66

APPENDIX pg. 67

Addressing Conflict in Christian Community ..... pg. 67
Commissioning of Wardens & Members of the Vestry .... pg. 70
ECF Vital Practices: Resources for Congregational Leaders .... pg. 70
Sample Vestry Job Descriptions .... pg. 71
Vestry Covenant .... pg. 76
Vestry Meetings: Consent Agendas .... pg. 77
Vestry Meetings: Sample Format .... pg. 78
Vestry Stewardship Statement .... pg. 80

EPISCOPAL CHURCH FOUNDATION

Mission

The mission of the Episcopal Church Foundation is to strengthen the leadership and financial capabilities of Episcopal congregations, dioceses, and related organizations to pursue their mission and ministry.

Vision

The vision for the Episcopal Church Foundation is to be a comprehensive and holistic resource that helps revitalize Episcopal communities of faith.

Impacts

ECF offers services to help Episcopal communities thrive in a changing world.

Our programs strengthen congregations, help envision new ministries, and provide the tools leaders need to succeed. All are shaped by our guiding principles:

- We equip and empower lay and clergy leaders, partnering to bring about transformation, renewal, and positive change

- We support healthy, vital, and vibrant Episcopal communities of faith

- We provide relevant and meaningful opportunities to live out Christian stewardship and effectively raise financial resources for ministry

We seek new, innovative, and mission-based ways to be The Episcopal Church of the future.

FOREWORD

On behalf of the Episcopal Church Foundation (ECF), I am pleased to present the fourth edition of the *Vestry Resource Guide*. An independent, lay-led organization, ECF helps Episcopal faith communities engage in visioning and planning, develop leadership, and raise resources for ministry.

Vestry service and other leadership roles at the congregational level are important, challenging, rewarding, and fulfilling work. This is also holy work and requires a vast array of skills and abilities from a diverse group of people who are faithful, committed, and open to the Spirit.

In developing this latest version of the *Vestry Resource Guide*, we spoke with dozens of congregations and hundreds of faithful Episcopalians who are seeking to build vital faith communities with the capacity to empower people to live out the gospel as Christian disciples. We received numerous comments, questions, and other feedback that helped shape the content of this revised guide; this information will also impact our other programs, products, and services.

This is what we have learned and are now sharing with you:

- The most dynamic congregations are those that identify, nurture, and support visionary leaders, especially vestry members, who are committed to the spiritual vitality of the congregation.

- In order to function, thrive, and grow, congregations need to embrace a leadership model that focuses on lay and clergy partnerships and a team approach to engaging in the work of ministry.

- In partnership with the clergy, vestries need to become the spiritual, missional, and strategic leaders of the congregation.

- In addition to exercising important fiduciary roles and responsibilities, vestries must engage in ongoing visioning and planning, leadership development, and identifying the resources necessary for local mission and ministry.

- Congregational leaders, especially vestries, want access to current, relevant, and practical tools and resources to support their work.

In response to these observations and premises, ECF has designed the new *Vestry Resource Guide* to help you lead your congregations in dynamic and innovative ways.

While the *Vestry Resource Guide* addresses the issues and concerns of parishes and missions of all sizes and configurations, ECF recognizes that most congregations in The Episcopal Church tend to be small (with an average Sunday attendance of one hundred or less) with limited paid or professional staff. Consequently, the *Vestry Resource Guide* is designed to meet the needs of all congregations, large and small.

Finally, the *Vestry Resource Guide* is just one of many tools, resources, and programs ECF provides to congregations, dioceses, and other faith communities throughout The Episcopal Church. We are especially excited and confident that this new edition will be a valuable resource to vestries and other leaders as you navigate the challenges, opportunities, and complexities of a changing church and world.

We pray for your continued strength, courage, vision, patience, inspiration, and joy as you embark on this leadership journey—discerning what God is calling you to be and do as the Body of Christ known as The Episcopal Church in your own particular time and place.

Faithfully,

Donald V. Romanik
President
Episcopal Church Foundation

ACKNOWLEDGMENTS

Editor

Nancy Davidge, associate program director, Episcopal Church Foundation, and editor, ECF Vital Practices

Writer

Susan Elliott, writer and former communications director, St. Columba's Episcopal Church, Washington, DC

Episcopal Church Foundation Leadership Resources team

- Miguel Escobar, senior program director
- Kate Adams, special projects director
- Ron Byrd, ECF Vital Teams lead consultant
- Brendon Hunter, associate program director
- Rosa Lindahl, ECF Vital Teams lead consultant

This revision is the result of many conversations with congregational leaders from across The Episcopal Church. Before changing a single word, we asked current and former vestry members, clergy, and diocesan staff to share what they see as the primary challenges and opportunities vestries face today. We asked if they were familiar with the *Vestry Resource Guide*, did they use it, and if so, what was valuable and what seemed out of date or unclear. We reviewed the feedback offered by ECF Vital Practices and *Vestry Papers* subscribers through our reader surveys as well as feedback from the ECF Vital Practices advisory committee.

We also queried our ECF leadership resources and financial services consultants about their experiences working with congregations, again listening for identified challenges and needs that the *Vestry Resource Guide* might address.

From these conversations and experiences, clear themes began to emerge; the result is this revised version of the *Vestry Resource Guide*. Thank you to all who contributed to this effort.

Special appreciation is offered to the individuals who served as readers or consultants and offered valuable feedback on our manuscript:

- Martha Goodwill, parish administration resource specialist, Episcopal Diocese of Southwest Florida
- Mary MacGregor, canon for evangelism and congregational development, Episcopal Diocese of Texas
- Demi Prentiss, ministry development and stewardship specialist, Denton, Texas
- Bob Schorr, manager of church plants and strategic development, Episcopal Diocese of Texas
- Deborah Shamlin, vestry member and former parish administrator, Canton, Ohio
- Margaret Sullivan, rector, St. Andrew's Episcopal Church, Walden, New York
- Anne Vickers, chief financial officer, Episcopal Diocese of Southwest Florida

Thanks to colleagues at the Episcopal Church Foundation for their expertise during the writing of this guide.

- Donald V. Romanik, president
- Louise Baietto, senior program director, strategic resources
- Linda Buskirk, capital campaign and strategic solutions consultant
- Terri Mathes, senior program director and capital campaign consultant
- Jim Murphy, managing program director, financial resources
- Leslie Pendleton, associate program director and capital campaign consultant
- Kenneth H. Quigley, program director, financial resources
- Erin Weber-Johnson, capital campaign consultant

And, thank you to all of the contributors to the earlier editions of the *Vestry Resource Guide* for providing a solid foundation on which to build.

PREFACE

You have been elected to serve on the vestry, called to leadership in your faith community. We thank you for saying "yes" to this call to serve the body of Christ through your church. The willing hearts and hands of God's people carry the light of Christ into the world in this and every age.

The catechism in *The Book of Common Prayer* says that the mission of the Church is "to restore all people to unity with God and each other in Christ." That broad, overarching purpose becomes more specific and individual when you gather with the vestry to consider where God is calling your faith community in this day and time. Whether your congregation is small—and 69 percent of Episcopal churches have an average Sunday attendance (ASA) of 100 or less—or large, like the 4 percent with an ASA of 300 or more (or somewhere in between), you will face similar challenges.[1]

The face of religion is changing in the twenty-first century. In the United States, Americans are increasingly switching religions or claiming no religious affiliation. The Judeo-Christian tradition is no longer the dominant cultural force. Membership in mainline Protestant churches is declining and aging. In The Episcopal Church, we are experiencing an increase in Latino and other ethnic or multicultural members and congregations as the population becomes more diverse. Emerging church initiatives, nontraditional models—with proactive bishops and church leaders—are testing new ways to reach out to those who are disaffected or indifferent to Christianity. Changes in patterns of giving, diminished financial resources, and the costs of supporting existing buildings are providing significant challenges to many congregations. There is a growing recognition of the need for effective lay leadership at all levels of the Church. An increasing number of small churches are managing—some of them quite well—with part-time clergy.

What does this mean for you as a congregational leader? It means seeing incredible, surprising possibilities in the challenges. It means overcoming the all-too-human resistance to change and to boldly try new things. It means opening up to what the Spirit has to say through the people and community you serve. It means sharing your gifts with abandon. You have been called to service at a time when our faith communities need leaders willing to say yes to God—men and women who can build a shared sense of purpose and articulate a compelling vision of the future—leaders just like you.

---

1. Episcopal Domestic Fast Facts Trends: 2009-2013, The Episcopal Church.

Developed by the Episcopal Church Foundation (ECF) for the leaders of Episcopal communities of faith, this fourth edition of the *Vestry Resource Guide* reflects the changing landscape of leadership and congregational development. In the past, many congregations operated with the priest as the central leader and the vestry in supporting roles. New models of ministry call for shared leadership, inviting clergy and lay leaders to serve together. Of course, Church canons (rules) dictate some roles to clergy and others to lay leaders—we also look to the baptismal covenant, which calls on all people to seek and serve Christ.

This new edition of the *Vestry Resource Guide* reflects the concept of shared ministry and emphasizes the role of the governing body in strengthening the leadership capacity of congregations. Chapters on vision and planning as well as building strong leadership teams reflect our work with congregations across the country. We've reorganized content relating to governance, administrative oversight, and stewardship, and included stories of congregations that have been willing to adapt and change. At the end of each chapter, there is a list of related resources.

For more than sixty years, Episcopal Church Foundation has been committed to strengthening the leadership and financial capabilities of Episcopal congregations, dioceses, and related organizations to pursue their mission and ministry. As a lay-led organization, we are guided by four key principles:

- We equip and empower lay and clergy leaders, partnering to bring about transformation, renewal, and positive change

- We help build healthy, vital, and vibrant Episcopal communities of faith

- We provide relevant and meaningful opportunities to live out Christian stewardship and effectively raise financial resources for ministry

- We seek new, innovative, and mission-based ways to be The Episcopal Church of the future

We are pleased to partner with Forward Movement, a ministry of The Episcopal Church, to produce and distribute the *Vestry Resource Guide*. Forward Movement shares a common vision of providing resources for discipleship and leadership.

The *Vestry Resource Guide* is designed to support and strengthen the leadership of all congregations and recognizes that the traditional parish model of a full-time rector and vestry is not the only way today's churches are organized. Congregations without a full-time priest are juggling roles formerly held by the rector. Paired congregations, clusters, and regional ministries are often led by joint governing bodies. Many dioceses support innovative team ministries focused on the ministry of all the baptized. Emergent churches and new faith community plants are developing alternative structures to support their life and mission. A congregation with mission status has a mission, executive, or bishop's committee. A cathedral is likely to have a chapter instead of (or in addition to) the congregation's vestry. If your congregation fits one of these other models, you will need to understand how your situation is different from that of a vestry. Diocesan canons and your congregation's bylaws are good places to begin that research.

Because the traditional model of a parish led by a rector and vestry remains the most common, this edition employs the language of rector and vestry, though we use "church," "congregation," and "faith community" in addition to parish. References to Episcopal communities of faith include Evangelical Lutheran Church in America (ELCA) and other denominations that worship with an Episcopal congregation.

Language aside, we hope this edition of the *Vestry Resource Guide* proves a good and useful companion throughout your vestry service. And we encourage you to explore resources beyond it, beginning with ECF's Vital Practices website (ecfvp.org), where you can subscribe for bimonthly emails and blogs and also search by topic to learn what other congregations are doing to solve the very issues you face. ECF also offers events and webinars geared to our mission. Forward Movement (forwardmovement.org) offers an array of resources, including daily devotions, Bible studies, and theological reflections. But do not stop here—there is a world of helpful resources, answers to questions, and inspiration, ready to be tapped.

Please Note:

All references to the canons of The Episcopal Church and applicable state and federal laws, including publications, advisories, and other provisions of the Internal Revenue Code and Social Security Act, are to those in effect as of July 1, 2014. All of these provisions can and do change from time to time. In publishing the *Vestry Resource Guide,* the Episcopal Church Foundation is not providing any legal, financial, or other professional advice. Please consult your attorney, diocesan chancellor, accountant, financial advisor, or other professional if you have specific questions or concerns relating to the applicable canons or state or federal statutes or regulations as they relate to your unique situation or that of your congregation, faith community, or diocese.

CHAPTER 1

THE MISSION-FOCUSED VESTRY

Election to the vestry is exciting—a sign of your congregation's confidence in you. But it can also be daunting. The challenges our churches face today can make a vestry person wonder at Jesus' promise that his yoke is easy and his burden is light. We at ECF are in agreement, though, with retired bishop Henry Parsley. He writes in a *Vestry Papers* article that he misses vestry meetings. "Vestries should be one of the most exciting ministries in the church—joyful, in fact," he writes. "Healthy, effective vestries make healthy, effective parishes. When rectors and vestries work together as a well-aligned team, extraordinary things happen for the mission of God."

VESTRY RESPONSIBILITIES

Vestry members are legal representatives and agents of a parish, charged with specific responsibilities by the canons of The Episcopal Church. They share leadership responsibilities with the rector. As legal representative and agent, the vestry functions much like the board of any nonprofit, with responsibility for finances and management of property and human resources. Many aspects of the vestry's role are defined by entities beyond the congregation—local, state, and federal laws, and diocesan and Episcopal Church canons—as well as by the church's own constitution and bylaws.

But your faith community is also where you wrestle with questions of faith and find meaning and purpose for your life. It's where life's small and large events are marked and celebrated. So there is an important element of shared life and purpose in vestry leadership. You're not just *elected* to the vestry; you are *called* to a sacred ministry in your faith community.

The Call to Vestry Service Today

In this time in the life of the Church, when laity and clergy are recognizing the benefits of shared leadership, your call means working collaboratively with fellow vestry members and the rector to create a vision and plan of action that reflects God's dream for the congregation. It means cultivating congregation-wide conversations about where God is calling your faith community. It means balancing your role in discerning God's mission and vision with sound stewardship of its property and resources.

BEING A VESTRY MEMBER IN TODAY'S CHURCH

The Episcopal Church reflects the sweeping changes in American life and culture in the twenty-first century. As the United States grows more diverse, so do our churches. The fastest-growing demographic in The Episcopal Church is Latino members, with Asian membership, particularly in the West, coming in second. Evolving digital communications are bringing new ways for congregations to build community, network, and explore their faith. Greater fluidity in religious choice brings us new members from a variety of faith traditions.

Less encouraging for the Church is the impact of economic and political change on our faith communities. Downward mobility makes it harder for members, particularly younger households, to give as generously as previous generations to support their congregations financially. Political divisions over health care, immigration, gay rights, racism, and the role of government spill over into our congregations and dioceses, sometimes creating divisions that obscure our vision as followers of Jesus. While the Church has an opportunity—and obligation—to be a prophetic voice for issues of social justice, these conversations are not easy and sometimes result in fracture or significant discord.

Photo by Eucharist, Katie Forsyth, 2013

In addition, American society is increasingly secular. It is becoming more acceptable to be atheist, agnostic, or to say you are spiritual but unaffiliated with any particular faith. A growing number of children are raised in homes that do not teach or practice any formal religion (13 percent of Millennials as opposed to 5 percent of Baby Boomers)[2]. We cannot assume adults who were raised in the Church will return as in past decades, or that those who join us have more than a passing knowledge of the Bible or a basic understanding of Christian beliefs.

What's A Vestry To Do?

As vestry members, we can wring our hands and bemoan the changes and challenges—or we can open our eyes to the hunger for meaning and the need in our communities and the world around us. We can roll up our sleeves and get to work on finding ways to live discipleship authentically and figuring out Jesus' mission for our congregations today.

At ECF we see many ways in which churches are doing just that. Laity and clergy are working in partnership to discern relevant visions for their congregations. Small churches, unable to retain full-time priests, are forming collaborative ministries with neighboring denominations. Multiracial and multiethnic congregations are finding ways to build relationships that honor their diversity. Struggling faith communities are developing leaner models of church and ministry that utilize the gifts and skills of all.

2.   "Born and Raised: More Americans Are Being Raised Without Religion and Choosing to Stay that Way" by Daniel Cox. Copyright ©2014 TheHuffingtonPost.com, Inc. huffingtonpost.com/daniel-cox/born-and-raised-more-amer_b_3682847.html

FOCUS ON THE MISSION & VISION OF THE CONGREGATION

The shared responsibilities of the vestry and the rector can be described roughly as

• Discernment of God's call

• Identification of new leaders

• Stewardship and development of resources

• Special duties when a congregation is without a rector

We are convinced that the most important of these is discernment. The primary tasks for a vestry are discerning what God is calling your faith community to do and articulating a hopeful vision of the church and the world as God's mission. A clear mission and strong vision create a firm foundation for your decisions and actions.

A New Kind of Leadership

Worried about replacing the leaky roof? Struggling to squeeze a little more out of the budget? Distracted by grumbling about the rector's pastoral style or the organist's hymn choices or the shortage of volunteers for church school?

The challenges we face today call for a new kind of leadership from our vestries, one that begins with asking questions: *Why? What does this have to do with Jesus? How do our efforts help us grow as followers of Christ?* Before the vestry can begin to answer these

questions, it needs to spend time building a strong and healthy lay and clergy team with the rector. It needs to devote an upfront portion of its time to prayer, scripture study, and worship. It needs to engage in open and honest dialogue and to listen deeply to one another, the congregation, and the community beyond the church walls.

When the vestry is able to do that, the Holy Spirit has the opportunity to be heard. Perceptions and ideas can begin to coalesce in a mission that makes sense for the congregation in this time and place, a mission that clearly has to do with Jesus and with helping its members grow as followers of Christ.

When we prayerfully ask and answer these questions, the challenges of tight budgets, leaky roofs, and community criticism can be seen in the light of Christ's own mission for your congregation. They can be understood in relation to a hopeful vision of your church's future.

We are not advocating a mission and vision carved on tablets of stone or placed prominently on your website and other communications for all time. We see the vestry's work in mission and vision to be ongoing and adaptive. The Spirit is ever on the move, and we are called always to be open to new directions, new possibilities, and new life.

BUILDING LEADERSHIP FOR TODAY & TOMORROW

Second only to discerning God's mission is the vestry's responsibility for raising up new leaders who can help carry that mission forward. And the good news in this more secular age, when church attendance is not considered mandatory, is that the people in our faith communities are there because they want to be. They are looking for ways to live Christ's love in the world—ready and eager to share their gifts. Many of them are great candidates for leadership in the community. They just need to be asked.

Your Role as Recruiter

The first step in raising up new leaders is to be an enthusiastic ambassador for the vestry's emerging mission and vision. You may or may not be comfortable talking to a packed room, but you can make yourself accessible and talk with members of the congregation informally. Tell them what you've learned and share the vestry's process and its hope. Then, spend some

time listening. Some will be anxious about change; others will be excited and energized. In that second group you'll find the leaders your church needs to keep moving forward.

The more diverse that group, the better. The church needs experienced leaders, and it needs beginners. It needs longtime Christians and people who have just walked in the door. It needs leaders from the congregation's heart and from its edges. It needs leaders who reflect the rich mix of the community.

Talk to people and learn what they care about. Learn about their skills and experience. Look beyond the usual suspects. Don't be afraid to take a chance on someone who is new to the community—maybe even new to the gospel. You can stay in touch and help them along. New leaders grow and flourish with a little coaching and support.

Small churches in Florida, Colorado, Oregon, and elsewhere are teaching us all the value of collaborative ministry. In some areas the goal is growth, and in others it is a matter of survival. But the lesson we take from their collaborative efforts is consistent and not a new idea at all—we are all part of Christ's body.

Congregations may define and develop collaborative ministry in different ways, based on their contexts and needs. Some congregations share clergy, even across denominations. Some team up on programs for adults or occasional worship. We see frequent collaboration on community outreach and youth groups. All are finding that working together brings new energy and vitality to their communities.

We encourage you to learn from these innovative faith communities and to watch for opportunities to partner with congregations in your diocese or deanery, as well as other faith communities and organizations in your area. You'll build new relationships and gain a broader understanding of the way in which we are all Christ's hands and feet in the world. A lesson from preschool still holds true in our churches today: we can do a lot more when we cooperate and work together.

A Blueprint for Change

One of the largest Episcopal/Anglican churches in Brooklyn, New York, St. Augustine's represents what can happen when the vestry and clergy work together as partners. Crippled by debt, with buildings in disrepair and membership dwindling, the rector and vestry of St. Augustine's resigned in 1998, enabling the bishop to step in and assume control of its affairs as an aided parish.

The congregation had struggled several times in the past and had been rescued in each instance by a strong rector. This time, working with the bishop, diocesan staff, and elders in their congregation, the members learned a new model for leadership, one in which they understood their role as full partners in making the decisions that shape their church's life and ministry. The interim priest appointed by the bishop fully supported the new model, promoting his belief in the importance of a strong lay and clergy leadership team as he visited and talked with parishioners.

As issues were identified and prioritized, the bishop appointed committees made up of longtime and newer members of the congregation. In partnership with the rector, they went to work on three primary areas of focus—spirituality and formation, mission and ministry, and management and finance. Meeting monthly, the committees drew on the skills and talents of the congregation and the neighboring community as they developed more organized ways to manage the church's affairs and established clear procedures for handling finances.

In 2003 St. Augustine's was restored to full parish status. Today it is a growing, vibrant community, engaged in serving and welcoming its surrounding community, involved in public advocacy, and active in all levels of The Episcopal Church. It is once again financially viable, and its buildings are in good repair. And it is a beacon for what strong lay and clergy teams can accomplish.

DISCUSSION QUESTIONS

What led you to vestry service?

What gifts do you bring? As you reflect on this question, think beyond your work-related skills to your interpersonal style, life management skills, personal strengths and weaknesses, as well as your spiritual gifts.

What is your understanding of what God is calling you, and your congregation, to do? How did it emerge? How does this understanding influence your congregation's direction?

What is your vestry's leadership style? How would you describe the relationship between the vestry and the rector? The vestry and the wardens? The wardens and the rector?

What issues are facing your vestry at this moment? What might happen if you started each conversation by asking: "Why? What does this have to do with Jesus? And how is this effort helping us to grow as followers of Christ?"

RELATED RESOURCES

Where do you begin to delve deeper into these topics? Or find the resources mentioned in this chapter? Here are some places to start:

Appendix, page 67

Look to your diocese for:
- Diocesan canons
- Forms, protocols, processes, and procedures specific to your diocese
- Resources related to congregational development

Look to the Episcopal Church Foundation (ECF) and ECF Vital Practices (ecfvp.org/vrg) for resources, webinars, and workshops related to:
- Collaboration and building vital teams
- Leadership
- Vestry responsibilities
- Vision and planning

Look to The Episcopal Church (episcopalchurch.org) for:
- The Canons and Constitution of The Episcopal Church
- Demographic information related to The Episcopal Church

Other resources:
- *Beyond the Baptismal Covenant* by Donald V. Romanik, Forward Movement, 2010.
- *My Church Is Not Dying: Episcopalians in the 21st Century* by Greg Garrett, Morehouse Publishing, 2015. ISBN: 9780819229342
- *Transforming Leadership* by Katherine Tyler Scott, Church Publishing, 2010. ISBN-13: 978-0-89869-599-1
- RenewalWorks, a ministry of Forward Movement that focuses on spiritual engagement to revitalize leaders and congregations (renewalworks.org)

CHAPTER 2

THE MINISTRY OF THE VESTRY:
Governance, Structure, & Selection

It's easy for a vestry to become mired in canonical and organizational details, neglecting more significant responsibilities for discerning God's call for the congregation and building up the body of Christ. Seminary professor Sheryl Kujawa-Holbrook encourages you to let the formal vestry duties and organization rest lightly on your shoulders and remain open to new and creative ways to build the life and mission of your faith community.

"Many stressed nonprofit organizations today, including churches, are now asking questions about the degree of governance the church requires; how do we balance the need for order by an equally strong need for creativity and risk-taking? Key to baptismal living in church governance is the acknowledgement that church structures have, at times, stifled the generosity of the Spirit with a need for control. This acknowledgement is in no way a criticism of the many who exercise profound ministries faithfully every day. But it does speak to the realities of many small congregations and dioceses where diminishing numbers face expanding workloads and feelings of frustration as they perpetuate models of governance that are outmoded and out of balance with the priorities of ministry and mission in a particular place."

– Sheryl Kujawa-Holbrook, priest, educator, and author, Claremont School of Theology

GOVERNANCE

Governance—the rules and practices that ensure accountability, fairness, and transparency in an organization—is a key responsibility of the vestry, and is so named in the canons of The Episcopal Church, as well as in diocesan and church constitutions and bylaws. In addition, state statutes may dictate specific responsibilities for a vestry as the governing board of a faith community. Each vestry member should have, at the very least, a copy of The Episcopal Church canons, their diocesan canons, and the congregation's bylaws. Consult with your diocese regarding state laws and regulations.

The canons of The Episcopal Church stipulate that the vestry shall:

- *"Be agents and legal representatives of the congregation in all matters concerning its corporate properties and the relations of the congregation to its clergy" (Title I. Canon 14, Section 2).*

- *Ensure that standard business methods, as outlined in The Episcopal Church's* Manual of Business Methods in Church Affairs, *will be observed (Title I. Canon 7, Section 1).*

- *When a congregation is without a rector, the officers of the vestry are responsible for the continuation of worship, including the calling of a new rector (Title III. Canon 9, Section 3).*

- *The vestry has responsibility for nominating persons for holy orders (Title III. Canon 5, Section 2).*

In its capacity as legal representatives and agents of a congregation, vestries must be aware of ongoing responsibilities and potential liabilities. Vestries and congregations can be held legally liable for any of the following:

- Accidents and other incidents occurring on church property or during church-sponsored activities

- Violation of fiduciary responsibilities, especially those related to finances

- Violations of contracts, leases, or other legal agreements

- Wrongful termination and other employment practices

- Discrimination and sexual harassment and misconduct

In very rare instances, individual members of vestries may be held personally liable for significant acts of malfeasance or willful misconduct. Because of potential liability, vestries should ensure that the congregation has adequate liability as well as directors' and officers' insurance coverage, including coverage for employment-related actions. These policies can provide coverage for actual claims as well as legal defense. To review your insurance coverage needs, speak with your diocesan administrator or insurance carrier. Another resource to turn to is The Church Insurance Company, a subsidiary of The Episcopal Church's Church Pension Group.

Beyond the Canons to Shared Ministry

In our work with vestries across the Church, ECF finds that mission-focused vestries reflect the larger role the laity plays in the congregation's mission and vision. In these faith communities, vestries are responsible for:

- Ongoing discernment of God's call and articulating the congregation's mission and vision in its unique location, at this particular moment in time

- Identifying new leaders for the congregation and for the wider Church, including the empowerment of lay leaders and nomination of candidates for holy orders

- Stewardship and growth of resources for the realization of the mission of the church, including ensuring that standard business methods are observed and serving as agents and legal representatives of the congregation in all matters concerning its corporate properties

- Special responsibilities during time of clergy transition including the continuation of worship and calling a new rector

The Role of the Rector

In congregations practicing shared leadership and working in partnership with the rector, it is essential to understand the canonical responsibilities assigned to rectors by The Episcopal Church. The rector's responsibilities include:

- Worship and spiritual life

- Selection and oversight of all assisting clergy

- Use and control of all buildings and furnishings, as delimited by the canons

- Education of all ages in the scriptures; the doctrine, discipline, and worship of the Church; and in the exercise of ministry as baptized persons

- Stewardship education for all ages

- Preparation for baptism, confirmation, reception, and reaffirmation

- Announcing the bishop's visit with the warden and the vestry and providing the bishop with information about the congregation's spiritual and temporal state

- Applying contributions not otherwise designated from one Sunday per month to charitable uses

- Reading communications from the House of Bishops at worship

- Recording all baptisms, marriages, confirmations, and burials in the congregation register

It's a daunting list, and it would be an interesting exercise to consider the ways the congregation can work with the rector to help fulfill it. Even though these are the responsibilities of the rector, that doesn't mean he or she is charged with carrying out these duties alone. Delegating tasks while retaining oversight is a common practice. From the vestry to Sunday School, youth groups and Bible studies to myriad committees and groups that support every facet of congregational life, the congregation provides leadership and support to build and strengthen the community. When a church does not have a full-time rector, responsibilities are further distributed to sustain the worship and life of the congregation. The life of a faith community is a shared enterprise, indeed.

VESTRY STRUCTURE

As the primary leadership body for Episcopal communities of faith, vestries are made up of elected members who serve for a specific period of time, often three years. Vestries consist of elected members, one or more wardens, a treasurer, and a secretary or clerk. The canons of The Episcopal Church leave guidance on vestry election, terms of office, eligibility for reelection, and vestry size to individual dioceses—another reason to keep a copy of your diocesan canons close at hand. The sections below follow models used in most dioceses. Should you have questions, consult your diocesan chancellor.

Vestry Size

Vestry size varies. For many congregations, a vestry of nine to fifteen members, including wardens, enables optimum participation and ease of decision-making. Small congregations sometimes find that a smaller vestry is more sustainable. In some dioceses, canons permit the "vestry of the whole" model, where the entire congregation of a small church meets to do the work of the vestry.

Terms of Office

Vestry members commonly serve staggered, three-year terms with one third of the body elected each year. Warden's terms may vary. Terms of office are specified in the congregation's bylaws and may be dictated by diocesan canons. The practice of incorporating new members each year brings fresh insights and ideas while experienced members provide continuity. It also creates a critical need to include orientation and team building each year in the months following an election. Occasionally, a vestry member is unable to complete his or her term, leaving a vacancy. Check your bylaws and talk with your diocese about filling open seats on the vestry.

Who Can Serve on the Vestry

While not a canonical requirement, it is standard practice for vestries to reflect the composition of their congregations. Perhaps there are members of your congregation who are overlooked for vestry service— new members, youth, seniors, racial and ethnic minorities, single, young adult, or LGBT (lesbian, gay, bisexual, or transgender) members. The vestry should reflect the varieties of experience, skills, and interests in your faith community. Fresh perspectives and new voices enrich vestry discussion and discernment.

Youth representation on vestries has been encouraged since General Convention 2009, and many churches have amended their bylaws to include a briefer term, usually one year, for a vestry representative of high school age. Because state law often requires all members of a governing board to be of legal age, diocesan canons and congregational bylaws generally prohibit youth representatives from voting on actions with legal implications. It is a good practice to know what your diocesan canons and bylaws say in this regard. Questions should be discussed with your diocesan chancellor.

Some vestries reserve seats for members of specific groups or committees, a practice we do not recommend. A member whose purpose is to represent a particular group or activity is not free to provide the visionary and practical leadership for the congregation as a whole, which is the work of the vestry.

When writing or revising the vestry service section of your congregation's bylaws, it is a good practice to consider whether employees who are members of the congregation, their family members, and the family members of the clergy should be eligible for vestry service, as well as whether more than one member of a family can serve at the same time. You might wish to avoid potential conflicts and boundary issues by including a provision in the bylaws making employees, their family members, clergy family members, and the family of sitting vestry members ineligible for election to the vestry.

Eligibility for Reelection

Congregational bylaws usually determine whether wardens and vestry members are eligible for reelection after serving one or more terms of office, unless otherwise specified by diocesan canons or state law. Taking time off between terms can help to prevent burnout and expand the congregation's leadership base.

VESTRY LEADERSHIP

Wardens

Wardens are elected members of the vestry with particular leadership responsibilities. Most congregations elect two, known as senior and junior wardens, though some use the terms "rector's warden" and "people's warden." The wardens' election or selection process varies significantly from one congregation to another and from one diocese to another, making it especially important that it be clearly communicated and understood by the faith community.

The wardens' roles vary too, depending on the culture and traditions of the congregation and the rector's style and needs. Generally, the wardens work as lay partners with the rector, often meeting weekly to discuss the small and large concerns of the parish.

When the congregation does not have a rector, the roles of the wardens become especially important. At such times the wardens:

- Function as the communication link with the diocese

- Convene and preside at vestry meetings

- Make provisions for Sunday worship

- Take responsibility for the administration and maintenance of the congregation's properties

- Act as custodians of the congregation's registers and records

Other Officers of the Vestry

A treasurer, a secretary, and/or a clerk complete the roster of vestry officers. Some large congregations include a chancellor or legal officer. Many vestries appoint these officers from the congregation, bringing more people into leadership roles. Some congregations elect an additional warden (an accounting warden) to serve as treasurer. The congregation's bylaws should indicate whether appointed officers have voting privileges or voice but no vote on matters before the vestry.

Executive Committee

Some vestries have an executive committee consisting of the rector, wardens, treasurer, clerk, and certain committee chairpersons. Often the role of an executive committee is to help set agendas for vestry meetings and to provide guidance, keeping the focus on the congregation's hopeful vision for the future. Except in extraordinary circumstances, an executive committee should guard against acting on behalf of the vestry.

Special Purpose Committees

Special purpose committees expand leadership in the congregation and enable the vestry to focus on its primary task of creating a vision and plan of action reflecting God's call for the church. A nominating committee meets annually to discern and select candidates for election to the vestry. An audit committee might ensure compliance with the financial practices prescribed by The Episcopal Church, the diocese, and external accountants. A finance committee can explore efficient ways to manage money and other assets. A building and grounds committee may plan and oversee repairs, maintenance, and improvements to the church's property.

Special committees permit the vestry to delegate some of its responsibilities. Working with clear boundaries and parameters, these committees further build leadership and allow the vestry to focus its energy on discerning God's mission and vision for the congregation.

BUILDING A HEALTHY VESTRY

Nomination Process

Whether your congregation holds a contested vestry election or elects a single slate of candidates, the nomination process is the critical first step toward building a healthy vestry. In the most common procedure, the congregational leaders form a nominating committee consisting of a few outgoing vestry members and other members representing the church's demographics (seniors, households with children, singles, young adults). The committee invites the congregation to submit names for consideration and then meets to discuss current leadership needs and create a list of potential candidates. The slate is created from those on the list who are willing to serve.

In dioceses where congregations have the option of adopting the "vestry of the whole" model, only the wardens are elected.

Some churches find that a well-communicated process involving prayer and discernment is a very effective way to recruit candidates for the ministry of the vestry. Key elements in the process are careful planning, clear communication of the qualities they seek in a vestry member, and one-on-one conversations by clergy and lay leaders with potential candidates from all walks of congregational life. Be especially deliberate in seeking out people who may not consider themselves leaders in a traditional sense but who may bring particular gifts of service, discernment, and insight. A traditional nominating committee may then select the candidates. Some churches, like Emmanuel Episcopal Church in Houston, Texas, hold open discernment sessions, inviting potential candidates and any others interested to learn about vestry service. The sessions describe the work of the vestry and criteria and expectations for its members. Participants are encouraged to put their names forward for vestry if they feel called.

Photo Courtesy of Diocese of Olympia

Elections

Elections for vestry members generally occur at a congregation's annual meeting. While the vestry is an elected body, a contested election may not be required. Some congregations choose to avoid the dynamics of winners and losers by presenting a single slate of candidates. Other congregations have adopted a practice of using a nominating committee to identify two candidates for every position and then ensuring that those not elected to the vestry are named to a different leadership positions such as chair of a committee. St. James Episcopal Church in Knoxville, Tennessee, with permission of the bishop, has changed its bylaws to permit selecting vestry members by lot, drawing from a basket that contains the names of prayerfully selected nominees at their annual meeting.

Vestries considering changes in the procedures for nominating and electing vestry need to first consult the congregation's bylaws and diocesan canons and then amend or revoke and replace the bylaws as necessary.

Annual Meetings

The annual meeting has important legal components dictated by state law and diocesan canons as well as individual congregational bylaws. These legal components may include:

- Requirements related to timing of meeting
- The requirement to hold elections for officers and members of the vestry
- Definitions of what constitutes a voting member
- Eligibility for nomination to vestry or office
- Requirements related to posting the warrant
- What constitutes a quorum
- Who presides
- Required reports

Annual meetings also are an opportunity to share stories of mission, bring the wider church into discussion about the vision, and to provide updates on the activities of key committees and organizations.

DISCUSSION QUESTIONS

The church-wide canons have little to say about the relationship between the vestry and the clergy. Among the joint responsibilities of vestries and clergy, which are strengths of your vestry? Weaknesses? What might be done to build on the strengths and address the weaknesses?

How involved is your vestry in the discernment of your congregation's mission and vision? How might increasing vestry involvement in this area impact your work as congregational leaders?

When was the last time your vestry reviewed the vestry service section of your congregation's bylaws? If it has been a while, consider setting aside time for a thorough review, evaluating how your present bylaws are supporting or hindering your ability to carry out your responsibilities.

How does your congregation approach the nomination process? How do you choose your vestry? Your officers? What are the benefits and limitations of your present methods? Would you consider trying one of the approaches described in this chapter? How might you adapt it to meet the needs of your congregation?

RELATED RESOURCES

Where do you begin to delve deeper into these topics? Or find the resources mentioned in this chapter? Here are some places to start:

Appendix: Sample vestry job descriptions, page 71

Look to your diocese or congregational records for:

• Congregational bylaws

• Diocesan canons

• Vestry training

Look to the Episcopal Church Foundation (ECF) and ECF Vital Practices (ecfvp.org/vrg) for resources, webinars, and workshops related to:

• All church vestry

• Covenants and norms

• Governance

• Lay and clergy leadership teams

• Position descriptions

• Senior wardens and treasurers

• Vestry nomination and election

Look to The Episcopal Church (episcopalchurch.org) for:

• The Constitution and Canons of The Episcopal Church

• The Episcopal Church's *Manual of Business Methods in Church Affairs*

Other resources:

• Covenants and norms: The Kaleidoscope Institute, "Holy Currencies." (kscopeinstitute.org)

CHAPTER 3

BUILDING STRONG LEADERSHIP TEAMS

You bring your faith, your gifts, and your experience in the church and the world to the vestry table—as do the rector and each of your vestry colleagues. This richness brings a wealth of possibilities, but forging an effective leadership team from the diversity of experience, personality, and gifts is no easy task. It is crucial, however, if you are to do the work that God has given you to do.

At ECF, we are convinced that strong lay and clergy teams are a critical need in the Church today. We find that partnerships between vestries and clergy are more adroit at making the strategic decisions that will move their congregations forward, whatever the church's size or situation. Vital teams that honor and use the gifts, experience, and potential of each lay and clergy member are better equipped to address the many challenges that face congregations today.

Creating a vibrant and vital vestry is an annual task that begins with the incorporation of newly elected members and moves through a fairly predictable cycle. In the early, formative days, members are getting to know one another and figuring out how they will work together. Struggle often follows this period, as both new and old members explore roles and power. Once roles, group norms, and expectations are established, the team can begin to work effectively together. Committed to its task and comfortable with one another, the vestry will continue to develop through the year until it is time to bid farewell to members completing their terms and prepare to begin again.

Whether they are elected by ballot or from a slate or chosen by lot, the incorporation of new members into the vestry brings both challenge and opportunity. The challenge is to bring new members into relationship with the group and up-to-speed on current issues and concerns so they can participate fully. The opportunity is to strengthen group processes by reviewing and refreshing the guidelines, norms, and covenants that support the vestry's life and work. A round of introductions at the first post-election meeting is not enough. Time—that precious commodity—needs to be given to new member incorporation each year.

Annual Vestry Orientation

There is no single way to approach any of the issues facing a vestry, and that is certainly true of new member incorporation. In a small church where everyone knows one another and is generally well-informed, the process can be informal. A review of recent vestry actions in the first meeting or in a conversation with a warden or other vestry member may provide adequate preparation. Larger and more diverse congregations will need to put more planning and structure into their annual vestry orientation. In both settings, it's helpful to give new members copies of the minutes and finance reports going back a year or two and to review significant issues and decisions with them, as well.

Photo by Mary W. Cox

Many churches plan a half-day or longer retreat during which the entire vestry can discuss the challenges and opportunities they see in their community and begin to build relationships and an understanding of their work together. Whatever form your vestry orientation takes, it needs to build relationships among new and continuing members, convey critical information about the state of the congregation and recent decisions, and establish or review group norms and covenants.

Guidelines—Group Norms & Vestry Covenants

Why spend time on group norms and vestry covenants? From biblical times to our own, God has used ordinary, flawed human beings to accomplish great things. Vestries are no different. Each member, including the rector, brings his or her own expectations, preconceptions, and anxieties to the vestry table. Norms, which deal with procedure, and covenants, concerned with behavior, help bring those disparate, individual expectations and anxieties into alignment, facilitating the group's work and relationships. They help build the trust and mutual respect that encourages all members to share their gifts and ideas. Norms and covenants strengthen the team's ability to make decisions and to accomplish great things in Jesus' name. Developing these norms and covenants together is an important element of healthy team formation.

If you already have established (written) group norms and a vestry covenant, an annual review for new members gives everyone a chance to talk about what is working and what is not. It also gives new members a voice and a stake in the guidelines. It's a good idea to keep group norms and vestry covenants simple. They're meant to create an environment of trust and respect, not a barrier to healthy debate or group process. Some issues to consider:

• Meetings (length, attendance, cell phone usage, agenda procedures)

• Discussion (listening, handling debate/disagreement, courtesy, respect)

- Confidentiality (balanced with the need for transparency)

- Accountability (everyone's responsibility)

Whether you have norms and a covenant in place or are just beginning that work, it is important that every member of the vestry, clergy and lay, is heard and willing to agree to the guidelines established. This will probably be your first decision as a new vestry, and it calls for consensus, not a simple up or down vote.

A Safe Place to Work Together

Effective teams need a safe and open work environment where all members can openly share their ideas, their concerns, and their hopes for the future. For a lay and clergy team, that means following the baptismal promise to love and value your neighbor as yourself so that no one is outside the circle that meets around the vestry table. Be careful to avoid "parking lot conversations." These may involve a few like-minded vestry members who discuss an issue outside of the meeting (perhaps even in the parking lot), and then push their agenda on the group. These conversations fail to value and trust the contributions of every member. A safe and open environment requires setting aside biases and working through control issues as well as answering important questions: *Who is in charge? What are the ground rules for our work together? How will we avoid bad behaviors like bullying?* Adding a brief (five minutes or less) evaluation session at the close of each vestry meeting is one strategy for increasing the vestry's skill in becoming a learning community.

Leader As Host, Not Hero

Whether led by the rector or by wardens, your vestry will grow in functionality, organization, and innovation if the leadership focuses on team building. This is different from the in-charge authority figure familiar to most of us, the heroic leader who will get us out of whatever mess we're in.

The leader as host:

- Understands that it takes the creativity and commitment of everyone to move forward

- Pays attention to group dynamics and guidelines

- Supports and encourages the team

- Helps the team learn from mistakes

- Measures and celebrates the team's progress

- Honors the goodwill, energy, and faith that the vestry brings to difficult decisions

Making the transition from hero to host can be difficult and isn't accomplished overnight. Congregational leaders need to believe—and continually remind others—that the success of this inclusive model of leadership relies on everyone's participation. The successful leader as host is a skilled convener who extends sincere invitations for participation, asks good questions, and supports risk taking and experimentation.[3]

Photo Courtesy of Kanuga Conference and Retreat Center

---

3. *Walk Out Walk On: A Learning Journey into Communities Daring to Live the Future Now.* Margaret Wheatley & Deborah Frieze. Berrett-Koehler Publishers, April 2011.

Photo by Mary W. Cox

Vestry Meetings That Work

If you shape your meetings, your meetings will shape you. If discernment of God's mission and vision is at the center of your work, you will not begin vestry meetings with the treasurer's report. You'll devote time at the start of each meeting to the spiritual practice of opening your hearts and minds to the Holy Spirit's leading. Then you'll spend the bulk of the meeting on strategic, big-picture concerns. Reports and business items will naturally move to the end of the agenda.

Hopefully, your adherence to group norms and covenants will promise an efficient meeting that begins and ends on time, with each member agreeing to be present and to arrive on time. It is a good practice to provide agendas ahead of the meeting, as well as written reports from the rector, finance committee, and other committees or ministries, so members can read them in preparation for the upcoming meeting. Some churches use a consent agenda, where items such as minutes and committee reports that are expected to pass easily without discussion, are distributed to members

several days ahead of the meeting. Members are asked to consider the materials prior to the meeting, where they will be approved without further explanation or discussion. If any member has questions or feels a consent agenda item needs discussion, he or she can ask in advance that it be moved onto the regular agenda. This technique avoids needless discussion and frees up time for more significant issues.

Traditionally, the rector chairs vestry meetings, but that is not a requirement. Some churches find it helpful to have a warden or vestry member preside, a practice that retired bishop Claude Payne of the Diocese of Texas recommends in his vestry training. Freed from that duty, the rector is able to listen more carefully to the proceedings. Listening is key for everyone—listening to one another in vestry meetings, to members of the faith community, to the wider church, and to the community beyond your church building.

New member incorporation, guidelines, shared spiritual practices, good meetings, and an open and safe environment lay the groundwork for a strong team. What might this vestry team look like in action? How does the team build on that good base in its work to discern God's vision and mission for the congregation, identify new leaders, steward and develop resources, and lead in the absence of a rector?

Focus on Mission & Delegate

There are lots of ways to become sidetracked, but the way forward is to put a major share of the vestry's time and energy into discerning a vision and mission for the faith community. Let that big-picture work guide your priorities and expectations for other efforts. Because you can't do it all, establish committees and working groups for tasks like the annual stewardship campaign, vestry nominations, or one-time projects such as refurbishing the church entryway or completing a building use survey. Working groups and committees reporting back regularly to the vestry help raise up new leaders and involve more members of the congregation. Be sure to properly empower these committees to act by being wary of the temptation to undermine the process by revisiting the question once a working group or committee has offered its findings.

Ready, Set, Decide

A vestry's work calls for decisions on a broad range of issues—large and small, simple and complex, controversial and straightforward. Each issue demands attention (some a great deal), and all benefit from a shared understanding of the decision-making process.

- Mission is key and it should guide information gathering and discussion, serving as a touchstone for decisions.

- Invite the Spirit into the process, especially on core issues that impact the congregation's mission. Engage in deep and prayerful listening. Seek consensus.

- Tailor your process to the issue. Simple, straightforward, or time-sensitive decisions call for a yea or nay vote. Those with greater impact deserve ample time, attention, and prayerful discernment, and will benefit from decision by consensus.

- Gather information, listen to the congregation, and invite stakeholders to share their ideas. Encourage vestry members to share relevant knowledge and experience.

- You don't need to decide everything. Groups, staff, and committees should have authority to plan and make day-to-day decisions about their programs.

- Communicate regularly with the congregation.

- Once a decision is made, support one another in that decision and move on to the next item.

Take Action & Measure Results

There's an oft-quoted riddle that begins with five frogs sitting on a log. Four decide to jump off. How many are left?

Five, it turns out. Deciding is not doing. It's just the first step.

All decisions require follow through, and the vestry needs to assign responsibility for those tasks. Big decisions (such as a change in staffing or worship times) require a well-constructed plan of action. The plan needs to include:

• Clear goals and expectations

• A timeline with defined milestones or checkpoints

• Regular communication to the congregation on goals and progress using multiple channels

• A method for seeking support from stakeholders and critics

• A method for selecting people for each task involved and holding them accountable

• A way to measure results and evaluate impact on the congregation

When the plan is successful, celebrate and give thanks. When it is not, dust yourselves off, learn from mistakes, and give thanks to God for second chances.

Communication Matters

At some point every vestry member hears something like this: "When did we decide to change the sign out front?" If you're communicating well, you'll be able to say, "Don't you remember hearing about that? We mentioned it in a forum…wrote about it in the newsletter…it's on our website…there's a photo on Facebook."

Vestry decisions and plans need to be communicated to the congregation in a timely manner, utilizing the types of communications channels favored by your members—written, spoken, email, social media, etc. Be forewarned: people will still miss a lot. Their lives are busy, and they are often distracted. With that in mind, keep regular vestry updates simple and straightforward.

When there are significant changes underway or in times of transition or particular anxiety in the community, communication needs to be stepped up and carefully coordinated. Information and updates need to be positive and truthful. Style and tone should reflect the congregation's hope and mission. It's also important at such times to gather the congregation's views and to listen to its members. The vestry needs to be visible, accessible, and "on message." Face-to-face conversation can be a great anxiety reducer.

Communication beyond the congregation matters, too. The vestry should be aware of the church's communication with the diocese and the community as their decisions and plans may generate a response from neighbors or others in the area. Signage, the congregation's website, brochures, and other publications with current information on worship services, building hours and activities, and access for people who are disabled should be clear, consistent, welcoming, and presented using language your neighbors will understand. In addition, the canons

require that the vestry and rector meet periodically with the bishop to discuss the congregation's life and ministry. It's easy for a busy congregation to lose touch with the diocese and the bishop, and these meetings help strengthen the connection with the diocese.

In addition to seeing communication as an administrative function—one that is designed primarily to inform about action items and decisions—communication is also a ministry. It is through sharing our stories of faith—our experiences of God working in and through us—that we become witnesses to each other and the world. If communication is only seen as an exchange of vestry minutes, then it will never become a vital tool for building up the Body of Christ.

Hold Yourselves Accountable

Despite the pressing issues that invariably accumulate over the year, the vestry needs to step back regularly to evaluate its work and health as a team. Ask:

- Are we firmly focused on mission?
- Are we moving forward on the goals and expectations we set?
- Where is there measurable progress?

- Where are we stuck?
- Are we honoring our group norms and vestry covenant?
- Do we deal directly with disagreement?
- How are we handling conflict?
- Do we enjoy one another, laugh, and have fun together?
- Are we too immersed in vestry concerns to draw strength and hope from worship?

Where you are falling short, work on ways to improve. Where there is progress, give yourselves a hearty pat on the back. Where there is trouble, commit to work through it together.

Growing Pains of Change & Success

The Spirit is full of energy and surprises. And there is no doubt that if your work to discern and move your mission forward takes off, you'll be in for an exciting period of growth and change—a result that is bound to create resistance in your faith community. When this happens, your task as congregation leaders shifts to helping the congregation deal with the disruption and discomfort that often accompanies new life.

Change always involves letting go of the way things were. It asks us to innovate, to rethink our roles and our sense of purpose. It might also make us uncomfortable. Your role as a vestry at such times is to remain firmly focused on mission, to be patient and hopeful with those struggling with transition, and to manage your own resistance, trusting in what fourteenth-century mystic Meister Eckhart called "the magic of beginnings."

SAYING THANK YOU

Each year, the vestry cycle comes full circle as some members complete their terms and new members come on board. It is time to celebrate the accomplishments of the past year and the particular contributions made by each member and a time to give thanks for the presence and contributions of outgoing members.

The last vestry meeting should give retiring members an opportunity to share their observations and suggestions, as well as their hope for the vestry's work going forward. They might also be asked to share their wisdom and experience with the newly formed vestry at the annual vestry retreat following the election. The congregation may publicly thank retiring vestry members at its annual meeting. Some churches decommission them in a regular Sunday service. Whatever you choose to do, it is an opportunity to mark an ending and a beginning with prayer and thanksgiving.

Focus On Mission & Delegate

It takes time and commitment to become the mission-focused discernment team that our churches need today. Here's what happened when the vestry at St. Matthew's Episcopal Church in St. Paul, Minnesota, put prayer and dwelling in scripture as the first item on its agenda:

"Our understanding and practice of communal discernment of what God is up to has evolved from an occasional activity to our primary calling and focus. In order to enable our vestry to focus on the larger, more complex adaptive challenges our faith community faces, we raised up a management team composed of people in our church with expertise in business and human resources. They are able to take many operational items off the vestry's plate so the vestry can focus on big-picture issues. We also tried to bump as many property matters as possible to a property team. While the vestry is ultimately responsible for allocating funds for maintenance of the buildings, we knew that we did not need to waste precious time deciding things like what color the parish hall should be, but rather to keep ourselves focused on a 'big issue' at each meeting."

DISCUSSION QUESTIONS

Every time someone new joins a group or a member leaves, the group changes, in effect, becoming a new group. How do you rate the effectiveness of your vestry orientation process? What's working well? What would you change and how?

In groups, it is not uncommon for a few individuals to dominate the conversation. What steps does—or might—your vestry take to ensure that all voices are heard?

How comfortable do you feel speaking up at vestry meetings? Does your comfort level change when you find yourself in a minority position? What steps might your vestry take to create an environment where everyone feels comfortable contributing?

You've held your annual orientation, established guidelines for working together, shared spiritual practices, and created an open and safe environment—you've established the foundation for a strong team. What safeguards have you—or might you—put in place to help you stay focused on the big-picture work, i.e. discerning a mission and vision for your faith community and letting that guide your priorities and expectations?

How frequently does your vestry step back to evaluate your work and health as a team? Consider setting aside time at a vestry meeting or retreat to consider the questions raised on page 23.

RELATED RESOURCES

Where do you begin to delve deeper into these topics? Or find the resources mentioned in this chapter? Here are some places to start:

- Appendix: A Vestry Covenant, page 76
- Appendix: Commissioning of wardens and members of the vestry, page 70
- Appendix: Consent Agendas, page 77
- Appendix: Sample outlines for vestry meetings, page 78

Look to your diocese for:

- Resources on congregational development
- Vestry training

Look to the Episcopal Church Foundation (ECF) and ECF Vital Practices (ecfvp.org/vrg) for resources, webinars, and workshops related to:

- Communicating change
- Covenants and norms
- Consent agendas
- Discerning mission and vision
- Evaluations and mutual ministry reviews
- Lay and clergy leadership teams
- Vestry meetings
- Vestry orientation and retreats

Other resources:

- *Behavioral Covenants in Congregations: A Handbook for Honoring Differences* by Gil Rendle, Alban Institute, 1998.

- Covenants and norms: The Kaleidoscope Institute, "Holy Currencies" (kscopeinstitute.org)

- Leadership Development Initiative (leadership-development-initiative.org)

- *The Five Dysfunctions of a Team: A Leadership Fable* by Patrick M. Lencioni, Jossey-Bass, April 2002. ISBN-13: 978-0787960759

- *Speaking Faithfully: Communications as Evangelism in a Noisy World* by Jim Naughton and Rebecca Wilson, Morehouse Publishing, 2012. ISBN-13: 978-0-8192-2810-9

- *The Word Made Fresh: Communicating Church and Faith Today* by Meredith Gould, Morehouse Publishing, 2008. ISBN-13: 978-0-8192-2285-5

CHAPTER 4

VISION & STRATEGIC THINKING

Vestries today need to see beyond the quick, technical fix and tackle the more complex issues that ultimately can strengthen the congregation. That slower, more difficult work of transformational leadership requires a shared understanding of what God is calling the community to do. And the path to that shared purpose begins with these questions: *Why? Why are we here, in this particular place? Why do we do what we do?* Like inquisitive two-year-olds, we ask these broad questions that will eventually to the real questions: *Where is Jesus in all this? What is he calling us to do?*

Exploring these questions together is life giving. It is a way to discover a clear understanding of your church's work and hope for the future. Shared understanding of spiritual purpose has the power to guide leadership and energize the congregation. It is transforming. In our work with congregations we see abundant evidence that the prayerful consideration of mission and vision can empower Episcopal communities of faith to embrace the challenges and possibilities of this time.

We see this in places like St. Matthew's Episcopal Church in St. Paul, Minnesota, where congregation-wide conversations led by the vestry and rector have developed a vision for their Christian life, "The Way of Jesus." Its eight themes—story, prayer, simplicity, discernment, reconciliation, hospitality, generosity, and gratitude—provide touchstones for St. Matthew's life and ministry and represent its way of being Christ in the world.

We see it in western Massachusetts, too, where the catastrophic expense of repairing a collapsed church wall and another congregation's call to pursue vital ministries led to the creation of a new congregation, Grace Church, formed from the members of St. James', Great Barrington, and St. George's, Lee. Both congregations sold buildings that were sapping their energy and resources and created a new, combined faith community that meets and worships in a public social hall. Energized and renewed, Grace's members run two food pantries and a community garden—bringing Christ's love and care to the need they see around them.

DISCERNING MISSION & VISION

ECF defines mission as what God is calling your congregation to do. We understand vision as a hopeful picture of the impact of your mission on the church and world in the future. Well aware of the tendency to spend too much time crafting beautifully worded mission and vision statements—and not enough time on implementation—we encourage vestries to remember that these statements are meant to serve, support, and inspire the congregation. They should not be static but should be subject to ongoing discernment and conversation (and perhaps never more than 85 percent perfected). It is vitally important that they reflect the faith community's shared understanding of its call and the imagined impact of its life and work in the future.

The Vestry's Role

Ongoing attention to mission and vision is critical as vestries navigate the complex challenges and opportunities before them, and these should be a part of every vestry meeting. That big-picture work gives each member a chance to step back and see the whole of the community's life in the light of God's call.

Some vestries are already doing this, but others leave that deep, foundational work of discernment for retreats, if they address it at all. If this is true for your vestry, begin slowly. Introduce a short period of prayer and Bible study at the beginning of your meetings. It may take a while, but you'll begin to see connections between your church's life today and the ancient stories of God's people.

If you've already done some work on mission and vision, dust it off, and spend some time discussing it at each meeting. You may find that it no longer fits or that it should be realigned to meet the needs and changes within and beyond your church. If you haven't worked to develop a clear mission and vision or if you stopped at a mission statement and never considered a vision for your future, now is the time to start.

The important thing is to consider what you're doing, why you're doing it, and where it is leading you, being mindful to listen carefully for the Spirit's guidance along the way. Spending time in this way at the start of meetings connects the budget, staff, building, and programmatic items to God's call to your faith community. It grounds your efforts as you confront issues and set goals, and it helps you think strategically.

If you are just beginning this work, there are various ways to go about it. You may want to form a small task force made up of lay, clergy, and staff leaders to design and lead the process. To keep the vestry engaged, it's a good idea to include the rector and a warden or vestry member on that team. Alternatively, you may decide to work with a consultant or facilitator. You may also decide that a simpler approach led by vestry members and the rector is best for your faith community.

Engaging the Congregation

Discernment of mission and vision doesn't end with the vestry. It offers an opportunity for conversation in the congregation about its day-to-day life and future. This is an important conversation to have annually (or every two or three years) to help renew and refresh your shared identity, purpose, and direction.

Whatever your process, you'll want to give people a chance to talk about what the church is doing now and what they sense God is calling them to do. You'll need to cultivate an open and accepting environment that encourages deep listening and values everyone's input. Conversation should consider your congregation's own life and mission and also the needs and opportunities in the surrounding neighborhood, city, or town.

The idea is to find out where there is meaning and purpose in your life together and to imagine how it will affect the future. Your mission—what God has called you to do—can be stated simply. It is a description of what your church does in your specific location within the larger community. Here are a few examples:

"As a community of faith we gather for meaningful worship; form faithful disciples; serve those in need; use our time, talents and treasure in service to God's kingdom; welcome everyone."

"Sharing Jesus with neighbors"

"While St. Matthew's may seem like several other churches in the Twin Cities area, we are particularly characterized by:

- *A desire to go deeper spiritually*

- *A global perspective*

- *Artistic expression*

- *Hospitality*

- *Community leadership"*

It is important when discussing mission to identify your ministry strengths. They are a bridge to the future and to discerning vision. You might ask:

- What are we doing well?

- What do we do that is distinctive or unique?

- How do we welcome and engage the community outside our church?

- How are we an asset in our local area?

With your ministry strengths defined, the next task is to imagine the ways your presence and mission can impact the future. Consider together:

- What do we hope for our faith community?

- What do we hope for our neighboring community?

- What are the needs, hopes, and fears in the wider community?

- How will faithful attention to our mission build our church community in the future and share Christ's love in the world?

It's okay to dream big. The Christian life is all about extravagant hope.

Less important is wordsmithing a beautifully crafted vision statement. Instead, consider reality-based answers to questions about your congregation's strengths and future.

In some ways, discerning your church's mission and vision is playing catch-up with the Spirit, which is always out ahead of us. If you listen well and faithfully, you'll find important insights into God's presence in your life and ministry—often from unexpected places and people. As you and your congregation explore your church's call and its hopeful future, you will discover strengths and passions, challenges, and dreams. From these come the shared understanding of your faith community's values, purpose, and call, which will enable your church to embrace each challenge and opportunity with courage and hope.

Communicating Vision

Clear and consistent communication is vital before, during, and after the mission/vision discernment process. You are working toward a shared understanding of the ways your church's day-to-day life carries Jesus' mission into the future. Here are a few things to consider:

- Keep communication simple and avoid insider talk. Make sure you can be understood by everyone—from longtime Episcopalians to those who may be new or unfamiliar with your church's faith, life, and language.

- Use robust language, lively metaphors, and images. You want to move hearts and imaginations to see possibilities and to hope for great things, even when facing difficult decisions.

- Use multiple platforms (sermons, church website, social media, etc.) to discuss and communicate your vision regularly. It's not enough to simply publish what you come up with in one place and forget it.

- Create opportunities to include members of the congregation in the broader conversation about vision. Listen to what people offer. Use what you hear to further shape the vision.

- Tell stories. Your mission and vision are reflected in everything you are doing.

VISION & STRATEGIC THINKING

Once your church understands what God is calling it to do, identifies its ministry strengths, and shares a hopeful vision for the future, it is time to translate discernment into action. In the past, vestries often began a lengthy strategic planning effort that would produce a long list of goals, neatly slotted into a timeline covering the next three, five, or even ten years. At ECF, we are seeing increasingly that many strategic plans generate too many goals and leave little room to adapt to unpredictable and changing circumstances. Congregations are finding that these three-to-five year plans are outdated and shelved almost as soon as they're drafted.

A more nimble model is needed to address the challenges of today's fast-paced world. For that reason, churches and other organizations are turning to strategic thinking—an ongoing, dynamic process that understands the need to embrace change in order to move forward. Strategic thinking focuses on developing effective strategies for a few goals rather than for many. It recognizes that there are challenges and opportunities that cannot be fully anticipated at the present time.

Strategic thinking is not about bringing a project or plan to successful completion. It's much more like being responsive to the Spirit's leading—letting your vision guide you toward seeing possibilities, trying things, keeping what works, and letting go of the rest.

How Strategic Thinking Works

Strategic thinking is a way to address the big-picture challenges progressively. The process begins with three steps:

- Identifying a few goals that are aligned with the organization's long-term vision

- Identifying potential strategies for reaching those goals

- Evaluating your potential long- and short-term strategies in light of mission, financial capacity, strengths, and other criteria

A wide net is cast to collect as many strategies as possible. Asking questions—including identifying the things you value most as a congregation—might help you select the best ideas for achieving the goals. As a strategy is implemented, it is evaluated. If it's not working, it is dropped. For example, to live into its vision, Christ Church, Pensacola, Florida, identified some priorities for strategic action. These goals included developing more robust marketing, determining the best use of some recent property acquisitions, and providing vital programs to reach youth and families.

With the economy still reeling from the 2008 downturn, Christ Church did not immediately jump into new expenditures to achieve the goals. However, the goals became a guiding force for the vestry, which reviewed them annually and worked to strengthen Christ Church's ability to achieve them.

The process of identifying goals, developing, testing, and evaluating strategies is continuous—enabling organizations to tackle complex challenges and move forward, one step at a time.

Strategic Thinking Begins with the Vestry

Strategic thinking is an effective model for confronting the tough choices our churches face today, and it works for faith communities of all sizes. If you've followed us this far, you're well on your way to using this model to address the challenges and opportunities before you. You have a strong lay and clergy vestry team focused on discernment. You have identified ministry strengths and discerned a hopeful vision of your church's impact on the future. Your congregation has participated in the discernment process and has a shared understanding of your church's mission, strengths, and vision. Your communications—from the pulpit to Facebook—reinforce that shared purpose.

Now you are ready to use the big-picture time in your vestry meetings to apply strategic thinking to an issue that goes beyond the day-to-day business of your faith community. Select a challenge facing your church, and consider it in the context of the faith community's vision for the future. Identify a few major goals for the next twelve to eighteen months that will begin to address the challenge.

Let's say the urban neighborhood around your congregation is changing. The demographics are shifting with younger adults moving into the area and aging empty-nesters moving away. Your church is becoming increasingly marginalized, almost invisible. Let's also imagine that an aspect of your church's hopeful vision is that it will become a congregation that reflects the diversity of the neighborhood. With that scenario, over the next twelve to eighteen months, your goals might be:

- To participate in the community as a congregation

- To make your worship and life more welcoming and accessible to younger adults

The Congregation's Role

In a strategic thinking model, the leadership doesn't have to generate all the ideas. So the next step is to frame your goals as questions and take them to the congregation: How can we participate as a congregation in the wider community and become more visible? What can we do to help our new neighbors feel welcome in our life and worship?

Invite everyone—core leaders, newcomers, youth, active and inactive members—to participate in brainstorming strategies on these two questions. Part of this brainstorming should include time in the wider community talking with people who are unfamiliar with the congregation and asking questions about their needs and desires for a community of faith. In that great harvest of ideas you'll find creative and innovative possibilities. You'll also gain the interest and support of the congregation—a vital element in moving toward the goals you select.

Developing a Strategic Filter

Brainstorming produces a lot of potential strategies. The question becomes, "How does the vestry evaluate the ideas collected during brainstorming?" To do that, you need a set of values—strategic criteria—to bring best ideas to the surface. Some suggested strategic criteria are mission and vision, uniqueness, financial sustainability, identity, and internal capacity. To apply them, look at each idea and ask:

- Does this support our mission and vision?

- Is it unique or does it duplicate others' work?

- Is it financially sustainable through potential gifts or fees?

- Is it consistent with our identity?

- Do we have the internal capacity to begin and sustain this initiative?

In discussing the potential strategies together, your vestry will find that some ideas meet all criteria and others fall short in one or two key areas. With this analysis in hand, the vestry will decide on one or two ideas to implement. Regular evaluation is critical. If a strategy is not working, learn from the experience and try something else.

Maybe your congregation is not ready for a coffee-shop ministry. Try a different way to show that you welcome and care about the new community. Offer a worship service on a Sunday evening or begin a Bible study geared to younger adults. Host some service projects and invite neighbors to participate. Establish a community garden that can meet the needs of an urban setting and provide an example of environmental stewardship.

Go where your vision and the energy of your people take you. The point is to keep working toward that hopeful future, one strategic step at a time.

LEADING CHANGE

Inevitably vestry leadership will encounter resistance when gathering the congregation to consider mission and vision. "Misty and misguided," critics will say, "distracts from more immediate problems." Resistance will rear its predictable head again in the strategic thinking process. "I think we should be doing 'A' or

'B' instead of wasting time on these strategies." And it will show up willy-nilly when you least expect it. Questioning leadership is a high art in American culture, and vestry members need to be thoughtful about how they intend to deal with it as a leadership body and personally.

Explain What You're Doing & Why

The congregation has a need and the right to know what you're doing and why. They are all members of Christ's body and stakeholders in your faith community. Clear, consistent, and redundant communication—using every communication tool from forums and sermons to published materials and plain old conversation—whittles away at misinformation and gossip. As you learn the value of discerning vision, teach it to others. As you choose goals aligned with the church's vision and strategies to pursue them, explain the thinking that has led to the vestry's decisions. Good communication builds trust.

Invite Key Leaders

The vestry and rector are not the only source of leadership in the congregation. Every congregation has members who have gained the community's trust and respect. They can help or hinder vestry actions. Find ways (informal and formal) to include them and seek their advice and support.

The Visioning Process: A Case Study

Sari Ateek, rector of St. John's, Norwood, in Bethesda, Maryland, feels that many vestries do not realize that they have the ability to make a real impact on the life and mission of their congregations. "They just deal with the buildings and the business of the church," he says, "but when you have a group of leaders who can dream about the future of the church, there's so much power in that."

In 2013, St. John's vestry began an in-depth visioning process designed to lead the congregation in dreaming about the future of their church. Their goal was to discern and articulate a vision that would guide the growing congregation in pursuing the focused, purpose-driven ministries and mission that God has in store for them.

From the beginning, the visioning process was grounded in prayer and reflection. In a sermon on God's call, Ateek invited the congregation to put their names forward if they were interested in serving on a team to discern a vision for St. John's. To select team members from the many names submitted, the vestry employed a discernment method, grounded in prayer and trust in the Spirit's leading.

The team (which also included the rector, the senior warden, and an additional vestry member) was commissioned before the congregation and charged by the vestry to carry out its work in five phases. The first included spiritual preparation, team building, and information gathering on vision and discernment practices and on the broader community. The second engaged the congregation in discerning its core identity, while the third explored the needs of the broader community, listening prayerfully for the places where the church's identity and the needs of the community connect.

A year into the vision process, the team is working on phase four—creating a draft vision statement that will be presented to the vestry and congregation for discussion. In the last phase, the final version will be submitted to the vestry, which will determine how best to interpret and apply it.

The team is working to help the congregation understand that the vision statement is not going to produce a strategic plan. "This is an evolving process that will give us a real focusing lens, a twenty-first-century tool, that can help us with the myriad things people want to do and all the requests from the community," says senior warden John Ross. "It's about change," he says, "and it's very exciting work. I don't think God wants us to be sitting back but pushing forward."

Be A Non-Anxious Listener

Cultivate confidence in the path and process the vestry is taking. Monitor your own anxiety and learn to listen respectfully to people's concerns. Offer clarity where there is confusion. Encourage patience and the willingness to take the long view where there is doubt. Help those who are critical or worried to know that there is room for diverse opinions—that their thoughts, and more importantly, presence and prayers are valued. Model Jesus' compassion for others and his unswerving passion for his mission.

Fail Fast & Move On

Remember that Jesus did not call us to be successful—he called us to be faithful. When your strategic testing fails (and if you are being imaginative and taking acceptable risks, it will, at least on one occasion), recognize the failure, adapt or discard the strategy, and keep moving toward your vision.

DISCUSSION QUESTIONS

What are your congregation's top three ministry strengths?

How does your congregation's mission and vision reflect those strengths?

What is your congregation's hopeful vision of its future? What is the impact you are striving to achieve?

If your congregation has a strategic plan, how frequently is it reviewed? What would it take for your vestry to adopt a strategic thinking process?

What do you understand as the difference between your hopeful vision, goals related to that vision, and strategies for achieving those goals?

RELATED RESOURCES

Where do you begin to delve deeper into these topics? Or find the resources mentioned in this chapter? Here are some places to start:

Look to your diocese for:
- Resources for congregational development
- Vestry training

Look to the Episcopal Church Foundation (ECF) and ECF Vital Practices (ecfvp.org/vrg) for resources, webinars, and workshops related to:
- Appreciative inquiry
- Communicating change
- Discerning mission and vision
- Leading change
- Strategic thinking
- Vision and planning

Other resources:
- *Cultivating the Missional Church: New Soil for Growing Vestries and Leaders* by Randolph C. Ferebee, Morehouse Publishing, 2012. ISBN-13: 978-0-8192-2823-9
- *Radical Welcome: Embracing God, The Other, and the Spirit of Transformation* by Stephanie Spellers, Church Publishing, 2006. ISBN-13: 978-0-89869-520-5
- *Reweaving the Sacred: A Practical Guide to Change and Growth for Challenged Congregations* by Carol Gallagher, Church Publishing, 2008. ISBN-13: 978-0-89869-588-5
- *Transforming Congregations* by James Lemler, Church Publishing, 2008. ISBN-13: 978-0-89869-584-7
- *Transforming Disciples* by Linda L. Grenz, Church Publishing, 2008. ISBN-13: 978-0-89869-598-4

CHAPTER 5

FINANCE & ADMINISTRATION

The topics discussed up to now—mission, structure and organization, team building, vision, and strategic thinking—look pretty much alike, whatever the size of your congregation. Things get a little more complicated when we consider the vestry's responsibilities for finances, human resources, and buildings. In large churches with paid staff, vestry duties are mostly geared to governance and oversight in these areas, i.e. holding the staff accountable for their management roles, making sure funds are used efficiently for the church's life and mission, and seeing that the church meets the canonical and legal requirements of the church and state. In small faith communities with few to no staff, the oversight and management roles often merge, with the vestry managing everything from the Sunday collection to paying taxes to maintaining the church's sidewalks.

The same standards apply whether exercising oversight or hands-on management. The vestry is responsible for ensuring that the rules and practices for managing the church's financial, personnel, and property resources are fair, transparent, and in compliance with state laws and church bylaws as well as diocesan and church-wide canons. The vestry does not need to manage everything, but it needs to know how the books are kept, the state of the church's finances in relation to the budget, the plan for the annual audit, who is managing the repairs to the roof, and much more. Where work is delegated—whether to staff, committees, commissions, or individuals—clear lines of authority and accountability need to be determined, agreed to, and acted upon.

For some vestry members, these fiduciary duties are a piece of cake—part of their everyday business life. Others find it easier to understand theology, human relations, or nearly anything other than taxes and financial statements. If you're that second person, don't hesitate to speak up and ask questions. Clarity and straightforward talk on church finances begin with the vestry.

Vestry financial oversight is a leadership function that directly impacts your church's future. It would be nice to think faith communities are immune to financial mismanagement, but that is not the case. You may know stories from your own congregation or other faith communities where (intentionally or through neglect) funds have gone missing, taxes have not been paid, or expenses have been poorly documented. Poor administration combined with a lack of accountability and transparency in financial matters directly undermines the congregation's trust and subverts the church's mission.

In the following sections, you'll find the directives from Title I, Canon 7 of The Episcopal Church canons and additional guidance. Financial management is a complex topic, and we encourage you to:

- Explore the *Manual of Business Methods in Church Affairs,* available from The Episcopal Church's website.

- Read your diocesan canons and congregational bylaws.

- Check out the resources at the end of this chapter.

- Ask questions. It is all too easy for vestry members to approve financial reports they do not understand and to avoid the discomfort of asking hard questions. The hard questions and their corresponding answers are necessary and vital to your church's health.

Good Financial Management Begins with the Budget

The church's annual budget is one of the most effective tools the vestry has for its role as fiduciary steward of the church's assets. Adding a percentage increase to last year's line items is not enough, though. You should have a budget planning process in place that combines your everyday income and expense information with what you are learning about where God is calling your faith community. The result is a realistic and balanced budget that supports your church's growing understanding of its mission and vision.

There are different approaches to this annual budgeting process. In smaller congregations, the rector, wardens (in the absence of full-time clergy), or treasurer will manage the budget formulation process. In larger churches, program and administrative staff will also be involved. Sometimes a finance committee or commission manages the effort. However organized, it is important to have a defined budgeting process that provides for clear delegation of responsibilities and a timeline for the task. Budget formulation should be based on priorities and basic premises set by the vestry and rector, guided by real financial data and input from program leaders and staff. Discussing the priorities that guide the budget process with the congregation, as well as your hopes and challenges, helps them understand and support the budget that is approved.

Some things to remember:

- Build a balanced budget that reflects your mission and fits your finances.

- A good rule of thumb is to make sure that 75 percent or more of your budget is funded from individual contributions. For small congregations, two-thirds of the budget should be funded from individual contributions.

- Incorporate expenses for maintenance and repair—sometimes this is done through the creation of a capital reserve fund.

- Think ahead about how you will manage cash flow needs.

- Make sure that safeguards are in place and enforced to prevent mismanagement of funds.

Sound Business Practices

When it comes to business practices, it is important that vestry members recognize that this work is guided by the canons of The Episcopal Church, diocesan canons, federal, and state laws. Here's what The Episcopal Church canons say:

> Funds held in trust, endowment and other permanent funds, and securities represented by physical evidence of ownership or indebtedness, shall be deposited with a National or State Bank, or a Diocesan Corporation, or with some other agency approved in writing by the Finance Committee or

the Department of Finance of the Diocese, under a deed of trust, agency or other depository agreement providing for at least two signatures on any order of withdrawal of such funds or securities. But this paragraph shall not apply to funds and securities refused by the depositories named as being too small for acceptance. Such small funds and securities shall be under the care of the persons or corporations properly responsible for them. This paragraph shall not be deemed to prohibit investments in securities issued in book entry form or other manner that dispenses with the delivery of a certificate evidencing the ownership of the securities or the indebtedness of the issuer.

> – Title I. Canon 7, Section 1b

> Records shall be made and kept of all trust and permanent funds showing at least the following:

> (1) Source and date.

> (2) Terms governing the use of principal and income.

> (3) To whom and how often reports of condition are to be made.

> (4) How the funds are invested.

> – Title I. Canon 7, Section 1c

> The fiscal year shall begin January 1.

> – Title I. Canon 7, Section 1j

Financial policies and procedures for everything from counting and depositing the offering to accounting, reporting, and implementing safeguards are critical, whatever the size of your faith community. Your church should have written fiscal policies and procedures that are reviewed annually. You also should provide training for employees and volunteers who work with church finances. Many dioceses conduct workshops or offer training on church finances and training. Policies and procedures must include appropriate safeguards protecting the integrity of the people responsible for the disbursement and transfer of congregational funds, documentation for all reimbursed expenses, and monthly review of all fund transfers and account balances.

In large congregations staff manages this process, along with oversight from a finance committee and the treasurer, who reports to the vestry. In a small church the vestry and the treasurer may manage everything. In either case, the vestry should know who is responsible for handling money, managing and documenting financial transactions, paying taxes, and arranging the annual audit. Standard business and accounting practices should be followed. The treasurer should provide concise monthly financial statements that include a balance sheet, an income statement, a cash flow statement, and budget projections for each month.

Different Funds for Different Purposes

Vestry members need to know the names and functions of all funds maintained for the congregation, where they are deposited, and who has access to each account. Churches use various fund types to manage their assets:

- Unrestricted funds (general operating budget) may be used for any purpose designated by the vestry.

- Reserve funds are set aside by the vestry for specific purposes. Their purpose can be changed by vestry action.

- Restricted funds are designated by donors for specific purposes and must be used for those purposes. Examples include contributions raised for a building fund or a columbarium fund. They may also include a capital fund from which only the interest income may be spent.

- An endowment fund requires that the principal be maintained, with distributions made using either an "income only" or the more recently allowed "total return spending" policy. The endowment documents should give clear guidance on the purpose of the fund, whether it is restricted or unrestricted, and outline spending policies, purposes, and investment asset allocation. It is risky to use endowment income for general operating expenses—and all too common. If this is a practice in your congregation, your vestry's gift to the future could be to begin reducing the church's reliance on the endowment. The draw from the endowment might better be used to support a capital reserve fund.

- Savings accounts are often used for special or restricted funds. The accounts must be in the name of the church and not in the name of the treasurer or any other individual.

- Clergy discretionary funds are guided by diocesan canons. It is important to understand that they are parish funds, not personal accounts or additional compensation. The fund must be included in the annual audit and other financial reporting. Look to your diocese for guidelines as well as to the *Manual of Business Methods in Church Affairs*.

Taxes

Taxes are primarily the responsibility of the treasurer, but members of the vestry can be held liable for tax violations and should be familiar with the general requirements. While Episcopal congregations are tax-exempt organizations, they are still required to comply with federal laws for withholding and reporting employee income taxes and Social Security taxes. There are other situations (such as sales tax or unrelated business income) where your church may carry liability. To reduce your tax liability, we recommend that you use a payroll service rather than doing it in-house.

It is helpful to consult with appropriate professionals regarding your particular situation, starting with your diocesan finance officer. You can learn about federal reporting requirements for Episcopal churches and the Episcopal payroll services recommendations provided on the Church Pension Group website. (Please see *Related Resources*.)

Annual Audit

Here's what the canons say:

All accounts of the Diocese shall be audited annually by an independent Certified Public Accountant. All accounts of Parishes, Missions or other institutions shall be audited annually by an independent Certified Public Accountant, or independent Licensed Public Accountant, or such audit committee as shall be authorized by the Finance Committee, Department of Finance, or other appropriate diocesan authority.

– Title I. Canon 7, Section 1f

All reports of such audits, including any memorandum issued by the auditors or audit committee regarding internal controls or other accounting matters, together with a summary of action taken or proposed to be taken to correct deficiencies or implement recommendations contained in any such memorandum, shall be filed with the Bishop or Ecclesiastical Authority not later than 30 days following the date of such report, and in no event, not later than September 1 of each year, covering the financial reports of the previous calendar year.

– Title I. Canon 7, Section 1g

The annual audit, required of every congregation and submitted to the diocese, is an effective tool for the vestry's fiduciary role. It ensures that accounts and the treasurer's reporting are accurate; funds are safe and correctly allocated; financial policies, procedures, and record keeping are followed; and the flow of cash receipts and payments is controlled. Where needed, recommendations for improvements are provided. On occasion, the annual audit reveals a serious problem. But most often, the annual audit documents that sound financial practices are being followed—a protection for all who handle your funds. That assurance enables the congregation to pursue its mission and vision with confidence in the accuracy and safety of its finances and those who manage them.

An audit by an outside certified public accountant (CPA) or licensed public accountant (LPA) can be expensive, and some churches use a small team of experienced volunteers instead. As with an outside consultant, the volunteer auditing team requires access to the treasurer and to the business manager or administrator, neither of whom can serve on the team. Some small congregations share auditing teams of qualified individuals—another way that working together can help our faith communities. Using an outside firm that is experienced with church audits can also help reduce costs. Some offer reduced rates to nonprofits or even work *pro bono*, so it is worthwhile to explore your options. It is important to remember that **all** congregational funds need to be audited, including the clergy discretionary fund, thrift shops, preschools, etc., and not just those managed by the treasurer.

Insurance

Here's what the canons say:

> *Treasurers and custodians, other than banking institutions, shall be adequately bonded; except treasurers of funds that do not exceed five hundred dollars at any one time during the fiscal year.*

–Title I. Canon 7, Section 1d

> *All buildings and their contents shall be kept adequately insured.*

–Title I. Canon 7, Section 1h

Protection from fire, floods, and lawsuits is not in the Great Litany, but it should be in your insurance coverage. The canonical insurance requirements above represent the bare minimum coverage your church needs. A more comprehensive list would include:

Liability Insurance

- A base of at least $1 million of general liability for injury and property damage

- Director and officers insurance (D&O) to protect the vestry for its decisions on behalf of the church

- Employment practices liability in the event of allegations of wrongful termination, discrimination, and sexual harassment

- Educator's legal liability, if you have a school, to insure for claims against your teachers

- Worker's compensation, required by law for churches with one or more employees; it is recommended that churches carry coverage for clergy, even where it is optional

- Network security and privacy liability and media liability

Fiduciary Insurance/fidelity bonding

- In addition to the canonical requirement to provide a bond for the treasurer, the parish administrator, bookkeeper, and any other staff or volunteers who handle the church's money should be bonded. A blanket bond is often included in policies from The Church Insurance Company.

Auto Insurance

- Any automobile owned by a church or church organization should carry insurance with a policy limit of at least $1 million.

It is important to purchase adequate coverage. Strong internal controls and safeguards in business practices combined with proper maintenance and accident prevention programs can help reduce your risk and insurance costs. In exploring insurance, be wary of off-the-shelf business policies that may not fit your faith community. Your diocese can provide further guidance on insurance. The Church Insurance Company, a subsidiary of the Church Pension Group, also helps with assessing risk and provides cost-effective coverage for our churches.

Reporting

Here's what the canons say:

The Finance Committee or Department of Finance of the Diocese may require copies of any or all accounts described in this Section to be filed with it and shall report annually to the Convention of the Diocese upon its administration of this Canon.

– Title I. Canon 7, Section 1i

Reporting requirements are a reminder that your faith community is part of the larger Episcopal Church. The annual parochial report, compiled by each congregation for the diocesan bishop and the General Convention, is an important source of vital information on the life of the church. Your vestry will review and approve the parochial report each year before it is sent on to the diocese. Your diocese may also require additional reports as well.

PROPERTY MANAGEMENT

In addition to providing a place where the congregation can pray, learn, and grow in faith, our church buildings provide a visible presence and witness to Christ in their neighborhoods. They also serve the needs of the local area in a variety of ways. While some Episcopal faith communities find that their mission does not depend on owning buildings, the buildings and properties of most Episcopal congregations are a primary physical asset. The vestry is responsible for seeing that the building and grounds are managed and maintained.

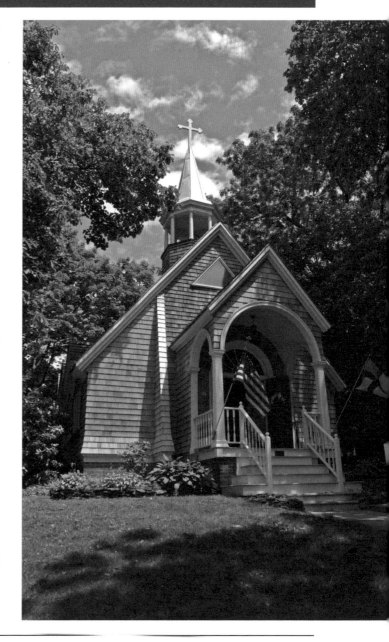

Two canonical rules have a bearing on the vestry's responsibility for church properties:

A vestry cannot "encumber or alienate" [or transfer or convey] any property without the written consent of the Bishop and the Standing Committee of the Diocese.

– Title I. Canon 7, Section 3 (summary)

All real and personal property held by or for the benefit of any Parish, Mission or Congregation is held in trust for this Church and the Diocese thereof in which such parish, mission or congregation is located. The existence of this trust, however, shall in no way limit the power and authority of the Parish, Mission or Congregation otherwise existing over such property so long as the particular Parish, Mission or Congregation remains a part of, and subject to, this Church and its Constitution and Canons.

- Title I. Canon 7, Section 4

Photo by Peggy Dahlberg

and to consider how the buildings might serve them better. Make sure that you're not spending time on issues that can be delegated to a property committee or a special task force. If you face a truly overwhelming need, your diocese can provide help and guidance.

A Few Building & Grounds Basics

In overseeing your church's buildings and properties, you should make sure:

- Appropriate contracts are in place.

- Maintenance expenses are adequately supported in the budget.

- Appropriate records are kept—including an up-to-date maintenance manual and an inventory of all church properties and their contents.

- There is planning for routine, major, and emergency repairs—such as a new roof or a replacement boiler.

- Safety is monitored, safety equipment maintained, and environmental hazards eliminated. The Church Pension Group and Church Insurance offer resources related to risk management.

- Safety and security procedures are in place.

- Insurance is adequate and reviewed and updated annually.

- Carefully considered policies for free and rental use of building space are in place.

It's important to pay careful attention when you contract with outside employers, especially in regard to their contractual liabilities. Make sure you use only licensed and insured contractors. Unpaid volunteers are covered by your general liability insurance.

As with finances, in mid-to-large congregations, staff generally handles building management and maintenance. In small congregations, the vestry may do that work themselves with the congregation's help. In churches of any size, the vestry often creates a buildings and grounds or property committee to monitor care standards and maintenance requirements and plan for building needs. The committee reports to the vestry.

Your Buildings Have a Mission

With or without building staff and a property committee, it is easy for the vestry to get stuck in the knotty details of building maintenance, safety, insurance, and terms of use. At such times, it's important to step back and use big-picture time in vestry meetings to reflect on how your buildings serve your mission and your hopeful vision of the future—

HUMAN RESOURCE MANAGEMENT

Human resource management is concerned with recruiting and hiring; compensation and benefits; compliance with fair labor practices and laws; and employee safety, training, and review. Legalities aside, this puts your congregation in alignment with the

baptismal promise to strive for justice and to respect the dignity of every human being. Good business practices and faithful discipleship come together in the way we treat our employees and our volunteers.

Photo Courtesy of TREC Conversation, Katie Forsyth

Valuing Employees

In churches with paid staff, the vestry is responsible for the welfare and safety of the ordained and lay employees of the congregation. These responsibilities include:

• Ensuring that all employees receive adequate salary and benefits for their position. The canons of The Episcopal Church direct congregations to provide equal access to and funding of health care plans for eligible clergy and lay employees. A canon related to pension coverage for lay and clergy employees is also in place.

• Ensuring that all employees have a clear understanding of their role through a job description or a letter of agreement, the equipment and training to do what is expected of them, and a process to ensure all employees (lay and clergy) receive regular feedback about their performance.

• Ensuring that all employees understand that they have the right to a workplace that is safe and free of harassment.

• Ensuring that children are safeguarded. Most dioceses and congregations require special training for those who work with children.

As a vestry member you do not need to manage these tasks but you need to ensure that they are being carried out.

Guidelines for compensation and benefits are typically outlined by diocesan employment policy. Check with your diocesan office to ensure that you are meeting the diocesan minimum standards for your employees and for help in navigating the differences between clergy and lay compensation packages.

Valuing Volunteers

Faith communities of all sizes are essentially volunteer organizations, and the vestry plays a role in seeing that volunteers are cared for and valued. It is easy to get caught up in worrying about whether you will have enough Sunday school teachers or if you can find someone to serve as treasurer. These concerns may cause you to miss the love and faithfulness of the volunteers who wash and iron altar linens, tend babies in the nursery, change light bulbs, shovel the walk, and plant tulip bulbs. Finding ways to thank people and honor their ministries is important (this is the job not only of the rector but also of the vestry). It is equally important to nurture new volunteers so that tasks undertaken with enthusiasm and dedication don't begin to feel like life sentences for longtime volunteers.

In churches without paid staff, the vestry is doubly challenged to recruit and oversee volunteers to manage the business end of church life. Finding people with the skills, talent, and commitment needed to manage the church's finances and property is crucial. In these settings, the vestry needs to walk a fine line that respects the contributions of these important volunteers while making sure they comply with standard business practices and church and diocesan canons and state laws. Provide a clear description of the jobs at the outset and assign a vestry member to provide help and answer questions when needed.

SAFEGUARDING OUR COMMUNITIES

Our churches promise people of all ages a safe place to gather with others and learn about the God who made and loves them. Keeping that promise—and insurance coverage for a variety of liabilities—means observing safe church policies and procedures.

Prevention of Sexual Misconduct

Sexual misconduct policies are usually set by the diocese and adopted by congregations and organizations. At a minimum the vestry needs to:

- Establish policies regarding sexual misconduct, appropriate employee and volunteer relations, etc., and procedures to respond to any complaints.

- Ensure that all employees and volunteers receive adequate and accurate information, comprehensive training in these policies and procedures, an explicit understanding about what constitutes inappropriate behavior, and full knowledge of the consequences for engaging in such behavior.

Photo ©Susan Marie Andersson, Grace Church, Bainbridge Island, WA

• Ensure adequate supervision and oversight are provided to anyone leading a group—especially a group that includes children and/or youth.

Your diocese will have the latest information on safe church policies. Training materials are available from the Church Pension Fund's "Safeguarding God's People" series.

Alcohol & Tobacco Policies

Clear policies regarding the use of alcohol and tobacco at church events are also a safety concern. The vestry should make sure that such policies are in place, and that these policies consider the safety of children and include the provision of equally attractive and immediately available alternate beverages at all church events.

Rookie Treasurer

"The treasurer role can and should be as a top advisor to the church leadership," writes Tyler Schleicher in an article on ECF's Vital Practices website. "It should not be looked at as a check-writer and offertory counter."

Schleicher should know. When he became treasurer for St. Anne's in Ankeny, Iowa, he was faced with outdated and inadequate accounting software and a staggering list of duties that included:

- Weekly responsibility for deposits, offertory tracking, check writing, bill paying, account monitoring, and transfers to/from savings

- Monthly completion of vestry treasurer reports, bank reconciliation, and salary checks with appropriate withholdings

- Quarterly obligations for pledge statements and tax filings for employee tax withholdings

- Annual duties including the annual meeting treasurer report, W-2 forms to all employees, budget creation, parochial report filing (financial portion), and ensuring completion of annual audit

Schleicher began researching software for accounting and tracking pledges. He moved the church's finances to two reasonably priced, easily learned, and well-supported applications. His next big step—implementing automatic withdrawal—made a big difference in pledge income and brought a new stability to the church's budget.

His third step was to find ways to delegate some of his tasks. Schleicher found a local accounting company to handle taxes and the end-of-year W-2 forms. When a secretary was hired a few years later, he began transitioning some of the weekly treasurer duties to her. He also delegated responsibility for counting the offertory to a vestry member—with appropriate safeguards to make sure that the count and deposit matched up after every collection was processed.

Obviously, it took Schleicher a while to whittle away at his long list of tasks, but once he'd completed the steps above, it was much more reasonable:

- Monthly vestry meeting treasurer reports and salary checks with appropriate withholdings

- Annual Meeting treasurer report, budget creation, parochial report filing (financial portion), and ensuring completion of annual audit

More importantly, he was able to put time into strategic tasks such as tracking giving trends and determining various costs. He was freed up to fulfill the treasurer's role as top financial advisor to the church leadership.

And he was also able to offer this important advice to struggling church treasurers everywhere:

- Identify and focus on those parts of the role that most matter to the health of your church

- Find the tools that make the job easier

- Do everything you can to make life easier for donors, and delegate tasks so you can focus on what matters

DISCUSSION QUESTIONS

How is your congregation's understanding of its mission and vision represented in your budgeting process? What steps might you take to develop a budget that reflects these values?

Does your congregation have an accounting policies and procedures manual unique to your church in addition to the *Manual of Business Methods in Church Affairs?* When was the last time it was reviewed and updated?

Are the financial statements of related non-worshiping entities (such as thrift shops, ECW, men's groups, preschools) reviewed by the vestry and included in year-end reporting, including the annual audit and parochial report filing?

In what ways are your church buildings serving your congregation's mission and hopeful vision for the future? How might they serve them better?

Are inventories (lists or video) of furnishings and equipment for insurance purposes current and complete?

Good business practices and faithful discipleship come together in the way we treat our employees and our volunteers. Are you treating your employees and volunteers in a fair and respectful manner? What is your practice for recognizing and thanking those who give service to the church?

RELATED RESOURCES

Where do you begin to delve deeper into these topics? Or find the resources mentioned in this chapter? Here are some places to start:

Look to the Church Pension Group (cpg.org) for:
- Federal reporting requirements for Episcopal churches
- *Guide to Human Resources Practices for Lay Employees in Episcopal Churches*
- Information and resources related to employee benefits (lay and clergy) and payroll services
- Information and resources related to insurance coverage, including risk management
- Safeguarding training programs

Look to your diocese for:
- Diocesan canons and information about state laws relating to church finance
- Forms and requirements related to finance and administration
- Information about audits and other required financial reporting
- Human resources questions
- Training related to finance and administration

Look to the Episcopal Church Foundation (ECF) and ECF Vital Practices (ecfvp.org/vrg) for resources, webinars, and workshops related to:
- Administration
- Audits
- Budgeting
- Buildings and grounds
- Finance
- Human resources
- Insurance
- Treasurers
- Volunteers

Look to The Episcopal Church (episcopalchurch.org) for:
- The Constitution and Canons of The Episcopal Church
- The Episcopal Church's *Manual of Business Methods in Church Affairs*

Other resources:
- *Back From the Dead* by Gerald W. Keucher, Morehouse Publishing, 2012. ISBN-13 978-0-8192-2806-2
- Episcopal Church Building Fund (ecbf.org)
- IRS: Tax information for churches and religious organizations (irs.gov/Charities-&-Non-Profits/Churches-&-Religious-Organizations)
- Partners for Sacred Spaces (sacredspaces.org)
- *Remember the Future: Financial Leadership and Asset Management for Congregations* by Gerald W. Keucher, Church Publishing, 2006. ISBN 0-89869-518X
- The Church Network (formerly National Association of Church Business Administrators) (nacba.net)

CHAPTER 6

STEWARDSHIP & VISION

We don't know if Jesus worried about money. We do know he saw the hunger of a great gathering of people who had come to hear him, that he fed them with five loaves and two fish, and afterward still had leftovers. That's a tricky gospel for vestry members, responsible for managing and developing their church's resources. It's the disciples who make sense here. It's late, and this is a desolate place. Send the people away so they can find food.

But Jesus is always focused on his mission, confident that God will provide. Jesus uses what the people have given, and it is more than enough.

This is a good stewardship message for vestries—a reminder that God will use the gifts of the people in our faith communities to do "more than all we can ask or imagine" (*Ephesians 3:20*). Your task as a vestry is to focus on your mission and vision. Be diligent in managing the property and resources in your care. Trust God and your congregation to provide the means to move toward the hopeful future you have discerned together.

Patterns for giving change as society changes, so it is not surprising that we see significant generational differences in commitment to stewardship. People born before 1942 are likely to give to their congregations from a sense of duty, but succeeding generations (from Baby Boomers to Millennials) bring new needs, experiences, and expectations to the church's stewardship efforts. Some expect transparency about finances and need to hear how their contributions make a difference. Others want to know that the church is a caring community and that giving is not an obligation. Still others are technology-savvy and looking for ways to be involved and to be heard. Economic anxiety cuts across all generations, making stewardship one more item in the long list of demands on one's time and money.

But Christians also understand practicing intentional stewardship can bring joy. Congregations find that when they see stewardship as a life practice rather than an obligation—as focused opportunity to grow as Christians—giving is transformed. And so are congregations, families, individuals, and the world.

Year 'round Stewardship Formation

When stewardship is understood as the right use of the resources God has given us, it touches all aspects of our lives. Forming good stewards becomes an integral part of the congregation's worship, education, community life, and mission. Relegating it to the annual pledge campaign means your leadership team misses rich opportunities to build stewardship formation into the church's life and programs throughout the year.

To help your congregation grow into faithful and generous stewards:

- Preach and teach stewardship as a Christian practice through sermons, book studies, rector's forums, Sunday school classes, and new member classes.

- Offer classes on managing finances and time to help members understand those issues in the context of their faith.

- Create opportunities for clergy, leaders, and others to share their stories about stewardship—how it undergirds our faith and attitudes toward giving.

- Provide clear, straightforward financial information and invite the congregation's ideas and questions on budget planning. Show how giving supports your congregation's internal and external ministries.

- Plan events and projects through the year where people can give time, talent, or financial support. Celebrate their efforts.

- Thank people often for their gifts of time and talent and money. Gratitude is the heart of stewardship.

- Establish the practice of drafting an annual vestry stewardship statement. Trinity Episcopal Church in Swanton, Vermont, presents theirs in the form of a collect:

> [We believe that] *God, who is the giver of every good gift, you are ever present in our lives and in the world. You act through us, your people, to care for and provide for everyone.*
>
> [We invite] *We pray for the courage to break out of our insecurity and fear around money as we deepen our understanding of our relationship to you and how we use our financial resources to do your work in the world.*
>
> [We commit] *We pray these things that we might know you better, that you will increase our desire and ability to give and help others through ministry and friendship and to gratefully commit ourselves to the work you have given us to do.* Amen.

Thanking the congregation for their gifts is a critical (and frequently missing) element in stewardship planning. A thank you letter is not enough. Sunday announcements, sermons, personal expressions of gratitude, newsletter articles, and special celebratory events are among the many meaningful ways to thank the members of your faith community for their expressions of stewardship. You might include a photo of a well-loved ministry or a beautifully designed card tucked into the quarterly pledge statement with a note of thanks, add a listing at the end of annual report with the names of everyone who has given time to each of your church's ministries, or host a party for volunteers—these are simple ways to thank people (personally and privately) for the ways they support your church's mission and vision.

Do It Your Way

Stewardship formation needs to be shaped to fit your faith community. In large churches, program planning for stewardship formation is often a clergy/staff function. In other congregations, the vestry might create a stewardship formation committee to coordinate programming throughout the year. Or your leadership team might make a start with a special committee, charged to find ways to recognize and celebrate stewards through the year. Encourage the committee to be creative. There are many ways to cultivate a culture that teaches, demonstrates, and celebrates faithful stewardship. Make a start and see what happens.

RESOURCES FOR TODAY & TOMORROW

Seeing that your church has the assets it needs for its life and mission are the primary goals of the vestry's fiduciary duties. It is also a common and understandable source of anxiety, whether your congregation is large and well resourced, a struggling new mission, or any of the myriad possibilities along that spectrum. Focusing on where God is leading allows church leaders to reframe financial assets as a powerful and adaptable tool for the day-in, day-out work of your church, a means for moving toward the hopeful future that you have discerned with the congregation. God will use what you have. You may face difficult decisions, but there, too, you're in God's good hands.

Episcopal congregations generally employ some or all of the following to generate assets:

- An annual pledge campaign to fund the operating budget

- Various income sources like consignment and gift shops, schools, building rentals, etc.

- Special fundraising efforts now and then for a particular project or need

- Occasional capital campaigns to support building maintenance/expansion, reduce or retire debt, encourage new ministries, and other purposes

- Endowments and planned giving efforts to fund future mission and ministry

Photo courtesy of St. Aidan's Episcopal Church, Alexandria, VA

As with other fiduciary responsibilities, the vestry does not need to organize and lead every fundraising effort, but you do need to provide strategic oversight, support, and leadership. You can help recruit people to serve on the committees that are needed and be willing to serve as vestry representative or in whatever ways you are needed. In some congregations, you will likely do much more.

Keep the Annual Pledge Campaign Focused on Mission & Vision

The annual pledge (or stewardship) campaign is a part of nearly all of our Episcopal faith communities. The temptation is to just go through the motions—mail a letter or brochure and a pledge card to each household on the register. But too often this practice misses the opportunity to underscore your church's mission and vision, remind members of what their faith community means in their lives, and show how their giving makes a difference. The annual stewardship campaign offers a chance to do something different—to catch people by surprise and open their eyes to God at work in their lives, their church, and the wider community.

While a stewardship committee usually plans and coordinates the annual pledge drive, your role as a vestry member is to provide support and encouragement.

• Remember there are many different strategies for an annual campaign. Some congregations are so thoroughly formed in stewardship that they operate without a strategy. Help your leaders explore options.

• Provide accurate and clear data on the challenges and possibilities facing your faith community.

• Make certain that campaign materials and presentations reflect your church's mission and vision. Consider online giving, if it is not yet implemented for your congregation.

• Consider including stewardship formation for children and youth and create at least one component of the campaign to speak to younger generations.

• Be ready to answer questions and willing to share your own experiences of giving to your church.

- Participate in stewardship dinners, neighborhood gatherings, Sunday forums, picnics, every member canvasses—whatever your church does to bring people together to talk about giving. Church leadership needs to be visible and supportive.

- Commit as a vestry to have 100 percent participation in pledging to the church. The amount pledged by each vestry member is a personal matter, but as leaders of the congregation, vestry members should model joyful and faithful giving.

It's important to remember that there is no one-size-fits-all stewardship campaign. Your pledge drive needs to fit your community. It should celebrate the varied gifts that support your church's life and mission, inviting members to offer time and skills as well as financial resources. The point is to provide opportunities for members to give back to God through your church community and for you to receive their gifts gladly and gratefully.

Capital Campaigns

Your congregation has grown beyond your building and it's time to expand. You can no longer delay replacing that leaky roof. Your church's debt load is stifling your ministries and dreams. These and other major financial needs can block a congregation's efforts to move forward. A capital campaign can raise the money needed to support your church's future life and ministry.

Vestries are often hesitant to consider capital campaigns, but at ECF, we see them as a way to raise up new leaders, create opportunities for mission and service, and build your congregation's financial capacity. We're convinced that vestries need not be timid about fundraising, even in tough economic times. Your congregation will respond to a clear need in the place that brings meaning to their lives. With prayer, a clear vision, and the support and involvement of the members of your faith community, you can accomplish great things.

A capital campaign generally involves three phases that can be described as discernment, feasibility, and giving. The first is perhaps the longest and most important: in discernment you identify a clear need, explore ways and costs to meet that need, study the available options, and develop a campaign plan. In each and every step of the discernment phase, the congregation is engaged, providing input, serving on committees, participating in discussions, and being informed through all communications platforms. In the next phase, a feasibility study determines whether the campaign can succeed. Once a feasible campaign plan and timeline are in place and approved by the vestry, the final giving phase begins.

Creating a capital campaign is an intensive, complex process, and even a relatively small campaign can benefit from professional consultation. While consultants will not solicit gifts (a responsibility that appropriately belongs to members of your faith community), they can organize your campaign calendar, train leadership and volunteers, assist in identifying and evaluating potential lead donors, coordinate preparation of materials, and offer guidance on fundamental decisions.

A successful capital campaign always accomplishes more than its purpose. It encourages the congregation to talk about possibilities instead of problems. It invites members to consider what God is doing in their lives and through their church to bring hope and healing to the world. It provides opportunities to celebrate the life of the faith community and its mission.

Special Fundraising Events & Projects

Street fairs, bazaars, yard sales, barbecues, auctions, and galas all fall under the special events umbrella. Special fundraisers that have gone on for many years often hold an important place in the community's heart. While some raise money for specific ministries, these events and projects generally take a great deal of effort and may not produce significant additional funds.

It's a good idea to think carefully before adding a special event or a new fundraising project to your church's program. Consider the activity in light of your

mission and its value to the community in addition to the dollars and cents it is expected to produce. Take a hard look at your established fundraisers now and then, too. If you're having difficulty finding people to run one, it may be time to let it go and make room for something new.

If an event builds your community, reaches out to the local area, enables your youth to go on a pilgrimage or mission trip, it may make sense. But if it saps energy better used for other ministries or more significant stewardship efforts, or if it bears little relationship to your church's mission, you may want to consider redirecting your efforts. Discernment may reveal other possibilities for achieving the same purposes.

Endowments Look to the Future

Churches are full of legacies. Our buildings, stories, and traditions—the very faith that we proclaim, and our mission in the world—all have been given into our care by those who preceded us. Even a new congregation builds on the zeal and missionary spirit of others.

Good stewards care about the future, and an endowment is a legacy for future generations. An endowment—invested funds that generate revenue, in perpetuity, for current and future needs—is a useful tool for small and large congregations. With one in place, a congregation has the means to accept and manage legacy gifts. An endowment can be started with any amount of money and built slowly. It's about the long view, not today's needs.

A well-structured endowment begins with a well-defined purpose. A critical decision is how the revenue will be used. It might support ministries beyond what is possible in the annual operating budget (as in a music or building endowment). It could be a source of "seed money" for new ministries. The more mission oriented the endowment's purpose, the more gifts it will attract. While some congregations elect to use endowment revenue to shore up the annual budget or as a rainy day savings account, this could be a recipe for future financial hardships.

An endowment needs to be carefully structured to honor its purpose. Once the purpose is in place, an enabling resolution sets up basic ground rules for how the endowment will operate and be managed. Usually a committee is appointed by the vestry to organize and oversee it. The committee enacts policies and guidelines for:

- Gift acceptance
- Investment
- Disposition of bequests
- Spending rules
- Designated gifts

Vestry oversight of endowments is a fiduciary responsibility, and great care must be exercised, whether creating a new endowment or managing endowments already in place. There are legal considerations and state laws governing endowment management and use. The investment goal and responsibility of the endowment

committee is to maintain the spending power of the endowment by following prudent investment and spending rules. It is illegal to spend revenue from a restricted or true endowment on anything other than its designated purpose or to invade its corpus. As with capital campaigns, you may benefit from professional consultation.

Whether you already have endowments in place or are starting one, remember that they are built through the gifts of the people. Keep good records. Honor the wishes of your donors. Tell what the endowment has done to all who will listen and explain how to give to it. And, as in all areas of stewardship, thank donors for their gifts.

Planned Giving

Estate planning, writing a will, and dealing with accumulated resources or assets are acts of stewardship as we confront the end of our lives. These are opportunities to give what we no longer need to the people and institutions we care about.

"Planned giving" is the term used to describe the ways money or assets can be left to your church upon your death, and how investment benefits can be given during your lifetime. It should not be seen simply as fundraising. Rather, it's a way to help members of your faith community see their accumulated resources or assets as an opportunity to continue the faithful stewardship that has marked their lives. It is a pastoral ministry that must always place the individual's interests and well-being first.

Planned gifts do not belong in the operating budget. They are given to support your congregation's future ministry. If you have an endowment, communicating its purpose, structure, and operation can reassure potential donors that their gifts will be invested to serve your congregation's hopeful vision into the future. If you do not have an endowment, you may wish to create one as part of your faith community's planned giving program.

A well-structured planned giving program carries profound benefits for the congregation by offering practical, faith-centered education and caring counsel to members as they confront the end of their lives. If you do not have a planned giving program, ECF and other organizations can help you create one.

You're Not in this Alone

Annual pledge campaigns, capital campaigns, endowments, and planned giving are important ways to build your congregation's resources. Some are more complicated than others. We encourage you to explore the resources and consulting services available for churches. Here are a few places to begin:

- Training, resources, and services available through your diocese

- Episcopal Church Foundation (episcopalfoundation.org)

- The Episcopal Network for Stewardship (TENS) (tens.org)

- Good Sense Movement (goodsensemovement.org)

- The Faith & Money Network (faithandmoneynetwork.org)

From Vision to Ministry

"People give to God through a parish's ministry," writes Neal Goldsborough, rector of Christ Church in Pensacola, Florida. "Having goals gives giving a focus."

Christ Church's work toward its current goals began three years earlier with congregation-wide discussions to identify the church's ministry strengths. Led by clergy and lay leaders, these conversations gave rise to a vision embraced by the entire congregation of a diverse and faithful community that welcomes and engages all people in a faith journey.

The church's next steps were to identify strategic priorities and goals aligned with their vision. And while the effects of the recession meant that some goals had to be postponed, Goldsborough describes them as a gift of hope that helped the congregation hold onto what they were called to do. "They helped us focus in the midst of keeping above water, so we could say, 'when the economy turns around, this is where we will go.'"

Today, as the economy recovers, Christ Church is once more moving forward toward the hopeful vision initially discerned. Goldsborough feels the strategic work on vision in the midst of the recession and the goals created set the stage for the increased giving that Christ Church is experiencing now.

DISCUSSION QUESTIONS

How do you see your vestry stewardship statement as related to your mission/vision statement?

What strategies might you use to increase the number of lay leaders who are involved in and passionate about stewardship?

How is your congregation planning for your financial future? How might a planned giving program help you meet your future goals? If plans are already in place, what is your process for measuring effectiveness of the plan in light of your congregation's mission and vision?

RELATED RESOURCES

Where do you begin to delve deeper into these topics? Or find the resources mentioned in this chapter? Here are some places to start:

Appendix: Vestry Stewardship Statement, page 80

Look to your diocese for:
• Diocesan canons and information about state laws relating to church finance
• Training

Look to the Episcopal Church Foundation (ECF) and ECF Vital Practices (ecfvp.org/vrg) for resources, webinars, and workshops related to:

• Annual campaigns
• Capital campaigns
• Endowments
• Budgeting
• *Funding Future Ministry: A Guide to Planned Giving,* Forward Movement, 2009.
• Planned giving
• Special fundraising events and projects
• Stewardship
• Year round stewardship formation

Look to The Episcopal Church (episcopalchurch.org) for:
• The Constitution and Canons of The Episcopal Church
• The Episcopal Church's *Manual of Business Methods in Church Affairs*

Other resources:
• Good Sense Movement (goodsensemovement.org/)
• *Remember the Future: Financial Leadership and Asset Management for Congregations* by Gerald W. Keucher, Church Publishing, 2006. ISBN 0-89869-518X
• "Stewardship in Hard Times" by Linda Grenz, Leader Resources (leaderresources.org/sites/default/files/Stewardship_in_Hard_Times.pdf)
• The Episcopal Network for Stewardship (TENS) (tens.org)
• The Faith and Money Network (faithandmoneynetwork.org)
• *A Spirituality of Fundraising* by Henri Nouwen, Upper Room, 2011. ISBN 10 083-581-0445.
• *Transforming Stewardship* by C.K. Robertson, Church Publishing, 2009. ISBN-13: 978-0-89869-607-3

CHAPTER 7

CLERGY TRANSITION

While choosing leadership for a church is similar to secular search processes in some ways, it is also vastly different. It is a spiritual process. It is a prime time for renewal in the congregation. It is a time when new leadership comes forth and new connections are made with the bishop and the wider diocesan community. It is also a time to review and restate the hopes and dreams of the parish.

– Gary Gleason, "I could fill this job in about a week!"

Your rector is leaving. Perhaps he has accepted a call to serve another congregation, or she is retiring. Maybe your faith community is moving from a full-time clergy position to part-time, or joining with another church to create a new congregation and call a new rector. It may be that the rector's departure is the result of conflict or a poor fit with your faith community.

Whatever the reason, clergy transitions shake things up and place particular demands on wardens and vestries. Clergy transitions challenge congregations and leaders to reflect deeply and prayerfully on who they are, what they have been in the past, and where God is leading them. These transitions offer a rich opportunity for your vestry and entire congregation to focus on vision and mission and to think even more deeply about what Jesus is calling your church to do and to become.

Topics we have discussed in previous chapters—ongoing discernment of mission and vision, a strong and vital vestry team, active recruitment of new leaders, responsible stewardship and development, and consistent communication will help make this transition a time of growth and renewal.

The vestry and wardens play a vital role in navigating the transition process. At his departure, the rector's canonical responsibilities for communication with the diocese, worship, vestry leadership, administration, and maintenance of the congregation's property transfer to the senior warden. During the transition, the wardens and vestry also work with the diocese to direct the process that will bring in a new clergy leader. Steps in that process include:

- Saying goodbye to the departing rector

- Providing for interim clergy leadership

- Establishing a search or calling committee

- Conducting a parish self study and preparing a parish profile

- Exploring potential candidates for rector and recommending a final candidate or candidates to the vestry

- Calling the new rector

- Welcoming the new rector and beginning to work together

Connected to the Diocese & the Wider Church

The first official task when a rector tenders her resignation is for the senior warden to notify the bishop. From that point, the bishop and the diocesan officer charged with transition ministry offer guidance and practical assistance. Procedures vary from diocese to diocese, and an early meeting with the bishop as well as regular communication with the diocesan transition office will help keep the process on track. Some dioceses provide opportunities for the leaders of parishes in transition to share resources and talk through challenges together. The Episcopal Church's Office for Transition Ministry (OTM) is another resource, particularly in identifying potential candidates.

If your congregation is considering a move from full- to part-time clergy leadership, the transition process will be different. The diocese needs to be informed before you make a final decision and may help you explore alternatives. If the move to part-time clergy remains the right choice, you will take a slightly different path through the steps of a typical clergy transition. Some dioceses, like the Diocese of North Carolina, are developing new models for helping faith communities transition to part-time clergy.

The day-to-day life in our congregations can make us forget that we are part of the much larger body of The Episcopal Church. The clergy transition process is a reminder that the life of every congregation is important to the whole Church. You're not on this journey alone. At the Prayers of the People in every celebration of the Eucharist at every Episcopal church, we pray for the whole Church. Those prayers are for your faith community too, now and always.

How Long Will this Take?

We could throw in a few statistics, but the truth is that the length of time a church is in transition is highly variable. A new rector could walk through the doors in six months to a year when:

- A congregation is well organized and healthy.

- The leave-taking is uncomplicated.

- Interim leadership is readily available.

- The search committee and diocese work well together and efficiently.

- The vestry's call is accepted by the candidate and approved by the bishop.

There are several places where that scenario can bog down, however. Sometimes there is significant work to do to rebuild a congregation, heal from anger or sorrow at the rector's departure, restructure systems where there has been dysfunction, or prepare for a shift from more than one to a single priest, or from full- to part-time clergy. The search committee can become stalled at any number of critical points in the process. Top candidates may accept other job offers. In any of those scenarios, it may take up to two years or more to call a new clergy leader.

Maybe it's not really about time but about taking a realistic look at your present situation and needs. Promise yourselves that you won't hurry or delay the transition process, and be intentional about taking full advantage of this opportunity to hold congregation-wide conversations about what you love and hope for in your church, the challenges it faces, and your expectations for your next clergy leader. These conversations are especially important when transitioning to part-time clergy or from multiple clergy to a single rector. What's essential in this process is that the position offered matches the congregation's expectations for its new priest.

A Few Basics to Keep in Mind

The challenges of leading during a clergy transition are real and unavoidable. Here are a few suggestions:

- Recommit to your vestry norms and covenants. Working together well is more important than ever during clergy transition.

Photo by Sing Baker, St. Andrew's, Encinitas, CA

- Keep prayer, Bible study, and discernment at the top of your vestry agenda.

- Monitor your own feelings and emotions. Make friends with them, as the Buddhists might say, and trust in what Teilhard de Chardin called "the slow work of God."

- Be a non-anxious listener. People need to share their feelings and concerns with their church's leadership. Just to be heard is reassuring.

- Trust the process you are in, trust others, trust God. Easier said than done, but do your best.

- Be proactive and collaborative in engaging any issues you encounter.

- Be mindful of who is designated as the congregation's ecclesiastical authority and come to a shared understanding of the roles and responsibilities of each and honoring the boundaries of each other's authority.

One final suggestion: communicate, communicate, communicate. Even when there is little actual news, the faith community needs to hear that the process to find new clergy leadership is moving forward and that their life and mission are in good hands.

Setting the stage for a healthy separation is an important first task for the wardens and vestry during clergy transition. The departure of a clergy leader ends a relationship. The rector has served as pastor, teacher, and spiritual guide, among other roles. Your clergy leader has baptized new members into the body of Christ, prayed for the dying, officiated at marriages, and broken the bread at the Eucharist and placed it in the hands of the worshiping community. There is depth and meaning in this relationship, and when you add the particular circumstances leading to the departure—retirement, conflict, a new job, elimination of a full-time clergy position, illness, or other possibilities—feelings in the congregation can run from grief to relief and everything in between. Good communication, a public celebration of the departing rector's ministry, and a smooth transfer of knowledge and responsibility to interim leadership can help your congregation let go of the past gracefully and gratefully and prepare for the changes ahead.

Open Communication is Key

From the first announcement of the rector's departure, the vestry, the senior warden, and the departing rector can help the congregation by providing clear, consistent, and open communication of the reasons for the departure along with information on how the church will celebrate and thank the rector and her family. A congregation-wide meeting with the bishop or diocesan transition officer to explain the transition process and timely sharing of plans for the interim can ease anxiety in the congregation. Regular communication in the months ahead on your church's website, in Sunday forums and announcements, newsletters, and social media is vital to keep the congregation informed and to reassure them that things are moving forward.

As in any time of change, it is important that the vestry and wardens make themselves available to answer questions and listen to people's stories, ideas, and concerns. You can help dispel rumors by providing consistent facts and as much transparency as possible. It's okay to simply listen, too. Addressing serious conflict or concerns needs to wait until after the rector's departure.

Celebrate the Departing Clergy's Ministry

Hold a festive reception after your rector's last Sunday service or another event that fits your congregation's culture and traditions. In addition, you may want to plan a series of gatherings to allow various ministries and groups to say goodbye. A loving farewell helps ease the pain of separation for both the faith community and the clergy leader and his family. It's more complicated to celebrate a pastoral relationship ending because of illness, conflict, or reduced clergy staffing, but it is still important. Your diocese can help in those circumstances.

Arrange for a Smooth Transfer of Responsibility

Clear and workable plans need to be in place to manage the worship, pastoral, administrative, and financial areas of your faith community's life. Before the rector leaves, the wardens need to:

Photo by Sing Baker, St. Andrew's, Encin

- Establish clear expectations for the church's future relationship with the departing rector and communicate them to the congregation. Generally such agreements prohibit the former rector from officiating at weddings, baptisms, or funerals and require the incumbent rector's permission for a return visit. Your diocese will have guidelines for this, as well.

- Arrange for a briefing from the departing rector on pastoral concerns and his connections with the diocese, community, and ecumenical groups.

- See that financial and parish records, signatory authority on accounts, and building use arrangements are updated.

- Assure that keys, credit cards, and other church assets are appropriately returned and documented. As appropriate, be sure that account user names and passwords are documented to assure continuing access for the congregation.

- Set up an exit interview to discuss the issues she has been handling, as well as her thoughts on what has been accomplished during her tenure and what she sees ahead for the congregation.

- Check in with committees to find out what they need to continue their work.

INTERIM LAY & CLERGY LEADERSHIP

Your church loses its primary staff member with the rector's departure, but its life and mission continue. Hiring an interim priest and building a strong lay and clergy team to manage both the ordinary and extraordinary demands of the months ahead are critical early transition tasks.

As in all aspects of the clergy transition process, your diocese has guidelines and procedures for interim clergy selection. That process generally begins after the rector's departure, though sometimes the interim is selected before the rector leaves. In some settings, the wardens, working with the executive committee or vestry, choose the interim clergy leader subject to the bishop's approval. In other cases, the bishop may appoint the interim rector or a priest-in-charge. Occasionally the diocese helps develop a plan for using supply clergy.

Dioceses often use priests who are specifically trained in assisting congregations with the challenges of an interim period. A priest who specializes in transitional ministry can help a congregation work through issues and identify weaknesses that may undermine a new rector if not addressed during the interim. She can help the faith community heal if there has been conflict because of the previous clergy leader.

Lay & Clergy Responsibilities During Clergy Transition

During the search for a new rector (described in the following section) the vestry, wardens, interim clergy, and staff manage the daily life and worship of the church, care for its people, and prepare for the next clergy leader. Here are some ways the vestry, working with the wardens and interim priest, can help the congregation make its way through a clergy transition.

- It is essential to continue paying careful attention to what you have been doing all along. The responsibilities of the vestry and wardens—ongoing discernment of God's call, raising up new leaders, and careful stewardship and development of the church's resources—are perhaps even more important during this time.

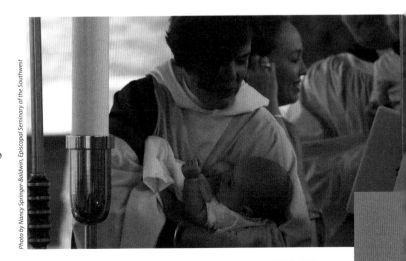

- If there is grief, anger, or conflict in the congregation, vestry members need to be part of the healing process. Support your interim priest's efforts to help your faith community let go of the past. Strive to be a visible, hopeful presence.

- Interim clergy and lay leaders walk a fine line between reassuring the congregation that what they love about their church will remain and encouraging members to be open to the possibilities that change can bring. Small adjustments to worship and programming (where needed) may help people see the positive aspects of change. Likewise, remember that stability matters to a congregation in transition and avoid making changes that do not grow out of the congregation's changing life together.

- The interim period between clergy leaders can be a good time to look at your organizational structure. Review your bylaws, committee structures, and staffing to determine what is outdated or not working. Fix what you can.

- Care for the members of your faith community. Listen to them. Be diligent and transparent in your work for them. Let them care for you, too.

- Keep prayer, corporate and private, a priority.

Sometimes the interim between clergy leaders permits new initiatives and even growth in the congregation's life and mission. Other transitional situations are about holding things together during difficult times. Do what fits your church and situation. Pray for your congregation. Leave the rest to God.

THE SEARCH PROCESS

Formation of a search committee (or in some dioceses, a calling committee) begins after the departure of the rector and is the responsibility of the vestry. (For simplicity, we will use the term "search committee.") While it is the vestry's responsibility to call the next clergy leader, the search committee carries out the search, from the initial self study and parish profile preparation to the recommendation of a final candidate or candidates to the vestry. The search for a new clergy leader is a complex process, and the diocese provides assistance, as does The Episcopal Church's Office for Transition Ministries (OTM). A search consultant, recommended by the diocese and hired by the vestry, may offer additional guidance and support.

The makeup of your search committee should reflect your faith community's diversity with regard to age, race, and gender. Often one or more vestry representatives serve on the committee, and sometimes there is also a youth representative. The goal in committee selection is to choose individuals who represent a breadth of personalities, leadership styles, and viewpoints; who have open hearts and minds; and who are committed to your faith community's mission and vision.

Along with a budget, the vestry presents a charge to the search committee describing the scope of the search and whether the committee is to present one candidate or several ranked or unranked candidates

Photo by Sing Baker, St. Andrew's, Encinta

for the vestry's selection. The search committee should be commissioned at a Sunday service and supported by the corporate and private prayers of the congregation. The search committee has taken on a big job, one that will require hard work, patience, and prayer. They will need to build themselves into a strong team with norms and covenants. They must be able to listen to one another, the congregation, those who present themselves as candidates, and the Spirit. The role of the vestry and interim clergy leader during the search is to encourage and support their efforts.

Parish Self Study & Profile

Before you talk about what you hope for in your next rector, you need to describe who you are as a faith community and where you believe God is leading you. The congregation's self study, designed to gather information for a profile of your parish and a separate Community Profile for the OTM, offers an important opportunity to renew discussion of your congregation's mission strengths and its hopeful vision for the future. The self study might include congregation-wide workshops employing Appreciative Inquiry or other techniques, interviews with leaders and members of the congregation, a review of your congregation's history, a study of the demographics of your local area, focus groups, or other approaches. Your diocese and search consultant will help with this.

The profile written from material gathered in the self study will provide a fuller, more accurate picture of your faith community's life and mission, as well as a description of your job opening and the qualities sought in candidates. Along with basic demographic information and an accurate statement about church finances, the profile should describe your church's worship style and theological positions and its hopes and vision for the future. It should talk about the neighborhood and larger community. In describing the rector you seek, the profile should be clear about the leadership style you want in your next clergy leader. Clergy leadership style was described as the most frequent source of serious conflict in congregations in the *2014 Episcopal Congregations Overview.*

Increasingly, parish profiles are published online, making them easily accessible and less expensive to produce. Some are quite elaborate, but whether your profile is published online with embedded video or as a simple print or online brochure, the goal is to present a true and lively picture of your community, with all of its challenges and its vision, one that will touch the heart of the priest who will be your next clergy leader.

The self study and profile are the search committee's responsibility, though they are sometimes delegated to the vestry or a separate profile committee. The vestry approves the profile, which must also be approved by the bishop before it is released. The diocese and sometimes the vestry assist the search committee in preparing the OTM's Community Profile.

Candidate Selection

When the OTM Community Profile and your parish profile have been approved by the vestry and the bishop, the position is posted and the search committee can begin to receive applications. In addition to applications from the OTM listing, the diocese, and sometimes ads in church publications, candidates suggested by parishioners or other contacts in the church may be invited to apply. Ask the diocesan transition officer if there are restrictions that prevent your interim priest or associate clergy from applying.

Photo Courtesy of Mary W. Cox/The Episcopal Diocese of Southeast Florida

Some dioceses require that all applications come through their transition ministry officer. Others allow applicants to work directly with the search committee.

From this point the search committee observes strict confidentiality regarding candidates, and communication with the vestry and the congregation can only touch on details like the number of applicants and where they are in the process. It is a time of waiting for the vestry and congregation. It's also an important time to pray for search committee members as they track and respond to applications and reduce the list of applicants to a manageable number.

Several steps and a great deal of labor later, the search committee arrives at a short list of candidates. That list is sent to the bishop for approval and in-person interviews begin, generally by a few committee members who travel to the candidate's current location. At the end of that step, a few candidates are brought in for interviews with the full committee, meetings with the vestry and the bishop, and a tour of the church and local area.

Most search committees hold a discernment retreat to decide which candidate or candidates to put forward to the vestry. There are times when the committee gets to this point and finds that none of the candidates are a fit for the congregation. As they pray and deliberate, the search committee needs to remain open to the possibility they may need to begin again.

The Vestry Decides

It is the vestry's canonical responsibility to call a new rector. After the search committee has made its recommendation, the vestry may choose to bring the final candidate or candidates in for another round of interviews before beginning its discernment process. The decision to call a clergy leader has great impact on a congregation's life and mission and should only be made by consensus and after deep and prayerful listening. If the vestry concludes that the recommended candidate(s) of the search committee will not be a good fit for the congregation, or if they cannot reach consensus, the search can be reopened.

When the vestry selects a new rector from the recommended candidate (or candidates), they notify the bishop and secure approval, then issue a call to the candidate. The vestry provides a full description of the rector's role and all financial matters and negotiates terms of agreement before the candidate's final acceptance. These details are included in a formal letter of agreement. Most dioceses have a template for such documents. The bishop receives a copy of the letter of agreement. In some dioceses, the bishop co-signs the original.

The search formally ends with the announcement of the new rector, and planning begins for a grateful farewell for the interim clergy leader and a warm welcome for the new rector.

The Search for Part-Time Clergy Leadership

If your church is moving to part-time clergy, your search process will be different and is likely to vary widely from diocese to diocese. The wardens and vestry may choose to lead the self study process and perhaps the search itself. Whoever leads the self study phase, congregation-wide conversation on mission and vision will be critical as you consider new ways to organize your church's life and ministry.

You will need to determine the number of hours a week or month your part-time clergy leader will work, what you want him or her to do, and then develop a plan for delegating the responsibilities that fall outside the clergy job description. Some things may need to be simplified or dropped. Focusing on your church's mission and vision can help guide those decisions.

The diocese can help you create a job description based on the profile that emerges from your self study and will publicize the position. You may want to convene a search committee to collect and review applications, communicate with candidates, and conduct interviews, as with a full-time rector search. Once the vestry or bishop's committee selects a final candidate, the bishop must approve the call before it is issued. The diocese will help create a letter of agreement, which is often co-signed by the bishop.

Some churches moving to part-time priests find a new understanding of what they want and need from their clergy leader. They are learning to take responsibility for planning worship, administration, and pastoral care. Their part-time clergy focus on spiritual formation, worship, and prayer, and nurturing the congregation's growth in Christian leadership within and beyond the community. It may not be the path your church would choose, but the Spirit works in and through us, whatever our circumstances.

A WARM WELCOME & A NEW BEGINNING

You've reached the final steps in the transition process, and you are preparing to welcome your new clergy leader, eager to begin work together and looking forward to a time when life in your faith community feels normal. Your new rector is in much the same place, often with the added complication of a move. Here are some ways the vestry can help:

- Form a transition team to help the new rector and her family get settled. The team might pull together a list of health care providers, veterinarians, banks, dry cleaners, etc., along with maps of the area and transit options. Its members could offer meals or move-in help for that first week and serve as an informal support group in the early months.

- Hold a congregation-wide welcoming event and arrange a series of smaller get-togethers to help the congregation and the rector begin to know one another.

- Build a history-sharing session around an evening potluck or a brunch following the Sunday service.

- Arrange a gathering where former senior and junior wardens can meet with the new rector and share their wisdom and experience. Encourage the rector to drop by committee meetings to meet the members and learn about their work.

- Be prepared to furnish background documents— vestry minutes, financial records, historical accounts, and such—to the incoming rector as requested.

Photo by Richard Snyder

Getting Off to a Good Start

Just as you schedule an annual orientation retreat with each new vestry, it is important to schedule a retreat for the vestry, wardens, and the new rector, preferably with an outside facilitator, soon after his arrival. It offers an opportunity to spend time together in conversation and prayer, to share your hopes for your working relationship, clarify how you will work together, and set goals for the year ahead—all important aspects of forming a new team. As you configure the retreat time, remember what you have learned about building strong lay and clergy teams—the importance of a focus on mission, prayer and Bible study, norms and covenants, a creative, open, and safe environment, the leader's role as host, dealing directly with disagreements, and facilitating good meetings. Find out what your rector has learned, too, about creating teams that work well together. She will bring new ideas and experience to share.

It will take time to integrate a new leader's style and ideas into your congregation's culture and approach. You're at the beginning of a relationship that will deepen over time, but there will be missteps, especially in the first months. It is helpful to schedule periodic, informal check-ins with the new rector to keep mission and ministry on track and keep everyone focused on the future.

An annual mutual ministry review invites the rector and vestry to reflect on how everyone is working together. With the emphasis on mutuality, this review is not about judgment but is focused on moving forward together toward a hopeful vision for your church's future. Are the vestry and rector meeting agreed-upon goals and expectations? Are we moving together or heading in different directions? Are the members of the team accountable to each other? Getting off to a good start with your new rector means planning a mutual ministry review for the end of your first year together and each year thereafter.

Plan a Glorious Celebration of this New Beginning

Soon after your new rector or part-time clergy leader arrives, you'll want to find a date to schedule the celebration of a new ministry. This date is often set in coordination with the bishop's office.

We're a liturgical church, and we believe that our processions, songs, prayers, preaching, and thanksgiving in Eucharist are more than words and actions. As you formally institute your priest as rector—or your part-time priest as your clergy leader—celebrate also the people young and old, those living and those among the cloud of witnesses, all those who have worked and prayed to bring you to this good day. Sing and pray with all your hearts, for God is doing a new thing.

Then roll up your sleeves and get to work—together.

Photo ©Susan Marie Andersson, Grace Church, Bainbridge Island

Your rector is leaving; your congregation is about to enter a period of transition. As a vestry, or individually, take a moment to think about a major transition in your personal life. Try to remember what you felt at that time. Were you anxious? Hopeful? Afraid? Where did you find support? What surprised you about the experience? What did you learn about yourself during this transition? What did you come to know about God during this experience?

How will you approach saying goodbye: as an individual, a member of the vestry, as a congregation?

How will your responsibilities as a vestry member change while your congregation is without a rector? What new things will you be accountable for? How might you support one another during this period of transition? What can you do to prevent vestry burnout?

What parts of the transition process, if any, seem daunting? What resources are available to you during this time from your diocese? Elsewhere?

Transitions in ordained leadership can produce anxiety in congregations. Suddenly there are many new questions: What will change? Who will replace the departing individual in the short and long term? How long will it take to find a replacement? What kind of changes might the interim and the new rector want to initiate? As the vestry, what approach will you take to minimize anxiety in your congregation?

What will be your instructions for the search committee? Who will lead the self study of the congregation? How can you best support the search committee's work?

Managing expectations is an important part of the transition process. How are you managing expectations related to timelines, expectations for the new call, and what will happen once the new rector arrives?

What might you do to help your new rector transition into the congregation? How can you help the new rector understand the congregation's traditions and expectations?

In what ways might the vestry facilitate the getting-to-know-you process between the new rector and his or her family and the congregation?

Where do you begin to delve deeper into these topics? Or find the resources mentioned in this chapter? Here are some places to start:

Look to your diocese for:

- Assistance in navigating the search process developed by your diocese
- Assistance in developing your parish self study and profile
- Mutual ministry review programs
- Programs, resources, or training offered to congregations engaged in the search process
- Resources related to mutual ministry or other congregational assessments

Look to the Episcopal Church Foundation (ECF) and ECF Vital Practices (ecfvp.org/vrg) for resources, webinars, and workshops related to:

- Change
- Clergy transition
- Mutual ministry reviews
- Vision and planning

Look to The Episcopal Church (episcopalchurch.org) for:

- Resources from the Office for Transition Ministry

Other resources:

- *Behavioral Covenants in Congregations: A Handbook for Honoring Differences* by Gil Rendle, Alban Institute, 1998. ISBN-13: 978-1566992091

APPENDIX

ADDRESSING CONFLICT IN CHRISTIAN COMMUNITY

The scriptures of the New Testament set high standards for how to conduct relationships in Christian community. For instance, James cautions believers to not favor the rich, to do good works, and to avoid judging others by the law. He also offers advice for the kind of Christian character that creates healthy community: "Everyone must be quick to hear, slow to speak and slow to anger; for anger does not achieve the righteousness of God" (*James 1:19-20*). Peter also encourages self-control, including controlling one's tongue, and lists similar guidelines for Christian community: "All of you, have unity of spirit, sympathy, love for one another, a tender heart, and a humble mind. Do not repay evil for evil or abuse for abuse; but, on the contrary, repay with a blessing. It is for this that you were called—that you might inherit a blessing" (*1 Peter 3:8-9*). The Pauline Epistles are full of guidelines for creating Christian community, including putting an end to slander, malice, abusive words, division, judgment, envy, and boastfulness.

These rules of conduct apply to all believers who gather in community. It would be a misapplication of these guidelines to say that one member had to suffer in Christian love and charity while another member persistently broke these rules by treating others with malice, envy, slander, or abuse. Those who claim to be Christians in community who do not obey the relationship guidelines of that Christian community are confronted.

The greatest guideline Paul offers to the Corinthian church—a community notorious for its need for guidelines—is love. But we misinterpret this love if it is just about feeling good, avoiding conflict, or being passive in one's behavior. Love is the means to Paul's greatest end, which is the "building up of the body." Everything is done for the community—the reception of spiritual gifts, their appropriate expression, the manner of ordering worship, meeting the needs of others, and the way we treat other members of Christ's body. Our management of community reflects that "God is a God not of disorder but of peace" (*1 Corinthians 14:33*).

Intentions also matter to Paul, because what we do in community reflects our true Christian commitment. Paul faults the Corinthians for bad community practices such as turning communion into a feast for the rich while the poor go without. He says that these actions are signs of division, factions, and lack of love, and Paul refuses to condone such behavior, "because when you come together it is not for the better but for the worse" (*1 Corinthians 11:17*). He does not counsel the poor to become better Christians in loving their abusers. Instead he suggests that those divisive members are undergoing a test, because through such actions "will it become clear who among you are genuine" (*1 Corinthians 11:19*).

The Pauline Epistles set guidelines for community behavior, especially emphasizing love, forgiveness, and community order—these goals are the goals of the whole of the worshiping community. The epistles, and especially those of Paul, offer little love or tolerance for those who refuse to live in harmony with others. The epistles are actually about Christian character in community. Those who cause problems in community are deemed not to be living by the standards of the whole community and are to be confronted.

How does Paul deal with the many community conflicts in his time? First, he believes the religious leaders have the responsibility to demonstrate these standards for how Christians treat each other in community. For Paul, that responsibility includes addressing the culture of how people are treating each other, such as "quarrelling, jealousy, anger, selfishness, slander, gossip, conceit, and disorder" (*2 Corinthians 12:20*). He believes that he and the leaders of that community have authority in directing its character, as long as they are focused on the building up of the community: "Everything we do, beloved, is for the sake of building you up. For I fear that when I come, I may find you not as I wish" (*2 Corinthians 12:19-20*). Paul appears sometimes so harsh to modern ears because he believes that confrontation is important to produce change. He does not confront simply to tell people off. He separates the Christian leader's responsibility to evoke godly grief that leads to challenge and change from worldly grief that only leads to depression or "death" (*2 Corinthians 7:9-13*). Even in separating people from the community, he encourages their return so that they do not completely lose heart. The hope is that the person will be reunited to the community.

Paul also suggests that there should be some kind of process of mediation at the community level to address conflict directly. He asks the Corinthians, "Can it be that there is no one among you wise enough to decide between one believer and another, but a believer goes to court against a believer—and before unbelievers at that?" (*1 Corinthians 6:5-6*). In the case of notorious sin, Paul also encourages the community to expel an unrepentant person so that he/she does not harm the community. But this is seen as a last resort. After a time of separation, Paul encourages the person to be reunited to the church community.

The Epistle to the Galatians shows us more clearly how confrontation should unfold in community: "My friends, if anyone is detected in a transgression, you who have received the Spirit should restore such a one in a spirit of gentleness. Take care that you yourselves are not tempted. Bear one another's burdens, and in this way you will fulfill the law of Christ. For if those who are nothing think they are something, they deceive themselves. All must test their own work; then that work, rather than their neighbor's work, will become a cause for pride. For all must carry their own loads" (*Galatians 6:1-6*). This suggests that while confrontation is necessary in

community, it must be done with gentleness, with a desire to bear another's burdens, and with an awareness of one's own shortcomings or sin.

Galatians offers this advice in the context of what it means for us to follow the commandment to love one another. We are to avoid controversies, divisions, or judgementalism because we are called to both freedom and to responsibility for the other. "For the whole law is summed up in a single commandment, 'You shall love your neighbor as yourself.' If, however, you bite and devour one another, take care that you are not consumed by one another" (*Galatians 5:14-15*). We follow that great commandment because we are now living by the Spirit. Rather than obeying the letter of the law, we form our actions through the gifts of the Spirit, which include love, joy, peace, patience, kindness, generosity, faithfulness, gentleness, and self-control (*Galatians 5:22-23*). But this is not a standard to accept abusive people's behavior. It still is important how we treat one another and form the character of the community, because "if we live by the Spirit, let us also be guided by the Spirit. Let us not become conceited, competing against one another, envying one another" (*Galatians 5:25-26*).

In Matthew's Gospel, Jesus sets out a process for dealing with community conflict.

In Matthew, the process of reconciliation takes three steps. First, to seek the offender out in private and confront them, pointing out the fault of their behavior against you. The second is to bring witnesses—others who have witnessed the behavior and can help the offender understand the behavior and its effects. The third is to bring the issue to the church—in other words, to the leaders of the church, to mediate the dispute. If the offender refuses to listen, they are to be ignored or placed out of the fellowship, suggested by the terms "Gentile and tax collector." One no longer has the responsibility to associate with them or seek reconciliation with them and can avoid contact with them.

So Matthew offers us a process, Corinthians offers us the ideal of community in order and love, and Galatians offers us a gentle way of seeking confrontation and leading through change. Refusing to accept a person who refuses to stop abusive behavior is an option in scripture. So is confrontation by the leader or leaders who seek to protect the good of the broader community. The guiding principle for conflict resolution is the preservation of the character of Christian community,

exemplified in the commandment to love as God loves us. No process, whether a tiered process of mediation or the direction of leadership, can occur without Galatians' corrective of gentle humility and the expression of the gifts of the Spirit.

Source: *Appendix A, "Fostering Respect in Church Settings" a report of the Dignity at Work Task Force, The Episcopal Diocese of Newark, January 2015, reprinted with permission.*

Related Resources

Where do you begin to delve deeper into this topic? Here are some places to start:

Look to your diocese for resources related to bullying, managing conflict, and signs of healthy church behaviors, including:

- The Episcopal Diocese of Chicago, Fierce Conversations and Thrive programs

- The Episcopal Diocese of Newark, "Fostering Respect in Church Settings" a report of the Dignity at Work Task Force

- The Episcopal Diocese of Texas, "Twelve Approaches to Healthy Congregations"

Look to the Episcopal Church Foundation (ECF) and ECF Vital Practices (ecfvp.org/topics) for resources, webinars, and workshops related to:

- Change
- Clergy transition
- Conflict
- Leadership

Other resources:

- *Behavioral Covenants in Congregations: A Handbook for Honoring Differences* by Gil Rendle, Alban Institute, 1998. ISBN-13: 978-1566992091

- *Discover Your Conflict Management Style* by Speed B. Leas, Alban Institute, 1998. ISBN-13: 978-1566991841 ISBN-10: 1566991846

- *Fighting With the Bible: Why Scripture Divides Us and How It Can Bring Us Together* by Donn Morgan, Seabury Books, 2007. ISBN-13: 978-1-59627-058-9 (Free study guide available)

- *Good News: A Scriptural Path to Reconciliation* by Steven Charleston, Forward Movement, 2014. ISBN 978-0-88028-381-6

- *How Your Church Family Works: Understanding Congregations as Emotional Systems* by Peter L. Steinke, Alban Institute, 1993. ISBN-13: 9781566991100 ISBN: 1566991102

- *Moving Your Church Through Conflict* by Speed B. Leas, Alban Institute, 1985. ISBN-10: 1566990122, ISBN-13: 978-1566990127

- *So You Think You Don't Know One? Addiction and Recovery in Clergy and Congregations* by Nancy Van Dyke Platt & Chilton R. Knudsen, Morehouse Publishing, 2010. ISBN-13: 978-0-8192-2412-5

Sponsor: I present to you *this person/these persons* to be admitted to the ministry of warden in this congregation.

Sponsor: I present to you *this person/these persons* to be admitted to the ministry of member of the vestry in this congregation.

Antiphon: The Lord gives wisdom; from the Lord's mouth come knowledge and understanding; the Lord stores up sound wisdom for the upright; the Lord is a shield to those who walk in integrity.

Officiant: I am your servant; grant me understanding

Response: That I may know your decrees.

Let us pray. (*Silence*)

O eternal God, the foundation of all wisdom and the source of all courage: Enlighten with your grace the wardens and vestry of this congregation, and so rule their minds, and guide their counsels, that in all things they may seek your glory and promote the mission of your Church; through Jesus Christ our Lord. *Amen.*

In the Name of God and of this congregation I commission you [*name*] as warden in this *parish* [*and* give you this _____ as a token of your ministry.]

In the Name of God and of this congregation I commission you [*name*] as a member of the vestry in this *parish* [*and* give you this _____ as a token of your ministry.]

From The Book of Occasional Services, © *2004 by the Church Pension Fund. Used by permission of Church Publishing Incorporated, New York, New York.*

Limitations of time and resources—as well as practicality—make it impossible to cover everything we'd like to in this edition of the *Vestry Resource Guide.* To delve deeper into any of the topics covered, visit ECF's Vital Practices website (ecfvp.org), a vibrant web-based resource for Episcopal leaders. Building upon the spiritually grounded, practical *Vestry Papers* articles, which have inspired and informed vestry members since 1995, ECF Vital Practices offers timely articles and resources to strengthen the leadership and financial capabilities of Episcopal congregations, dioceses, and related organizations to pursue their mission and ministry.

ECF Vital Practices provides a place for congregational, diocesan, and other leaders to share their stories, experiences, practical resources, and vital practices, as well as learn from one another. Vestry members are encouraged to become subscribers (it's free); you'll receive bimonthly emails and/or weekday blogs related to congregational leadership.

Content categories range from administration and advocacy to conflict and evangelism as well as hospitality, leadership, small church concerns, and more. Special focus is placed on five areas congregational leaders are most interested in:

- Change
- Communications
- Stewardship
- Vestry
- Vision & Planning

Key features include:

- Vestry Papers: themed articles relating to congregational vitality; published monthly

- Vital Posts blog: posts on faith, leadership, and stewardship by lay and clergy leaders from across our church

- Your Turn: practical resources developed and shared by congregational leaders

- Tools: practical resources developed by dioceses or organizations for congregations

- Webinars: online learning opportunities with expert facilitation and meaningful peer interaction

- Topics: search for articles and resources by topic

Resources are available in English and Spanish, with searchable indexes in both languages accessed through the Topics tab in the primary navigation bar.

SAMPLE VESTRY JOB DESCRIPTIONS

Congregations should have written job descriptions for every position, beginning with the rector and the vestry. Here we offer sample vestry job descriptions to customize for the needs of your faith community. We also recommend contacting your diocese for examples of job descriptions from other congregations or faith communities in your area.

General Job Descriptions For All Vestry Members

Vestry members should, to the best of their ability

- Have a love of God and demonstrate a commitment to following the way of Christ

- Be active in and knowledgeable about the congregation, its programs, and governance

- Be fair, interact well with people, and strive to earn the respect of the members of the congregation

- Commit themselves to the concept of partnership between vestry and clergy leaders, reminding themselves and others that the success of an inclusive model of leadership relies on everyone's participation

- Purposefully strive to be a servant of the people without the need to be the "most important" person in the congregation or the need to be the one with the right answers to everything

- Have enthusiasm and vitality for this ministry

Vestry members should be able to make the following time commitments

- Vestry meetings and committee work

- Vestry retreat(s)

- Weekly worship services, rotating occasionally if more than one is offered

- Congregational events: coffee hours, meals, fundraisers, Christian formation programs, etc.

- Diocesan meetings as necessary

- Annual meeting

Vestry members are responsible for

- Bringing one's whole self to the table: being present in mind, body, and spirit

- Risking openness with one's ideas, beliefs, and desires

- Offering talents to discern and support the congregation's mission and vision

- Being active ministers of the gospel in daily life and work

- Pledging financial support early in the annual or other campaign

- Praying daily for the rector, leaders, and members of the congregation

Senior Warden Job Description

The Canons of The Episcopal Church assign specific responsibilities to the senior warden and form the basis for their job description. These are in addition to the requirements and responsibilities of all vestry members.

Time commitment

- Weekly meetings with the rector, if required. These may be one-on-one or include the junior warden or church staff depending on the need of the congregation

Responsibilities

- Meet regularly with the rector to review the life and work of the congregation, plan ahead, and anticipate and resolve problems

- Provide leadership so the vestry can identify the mission, vision, and goals of the congregation; make and implement plans; assess programs; and celebrate achievements

- Provide leadership in the congregation by demonstrating a consistently positive attitude that seeks to resolve problems, recognizes accomplishments, and gives thanks for those things that build community and further the mission and vision of the church

- Be available to discuss any and all concerns with the rector and maintain confidentiality where appropriate

- Be available to discuss any and all concerns with members of the congregation; avoid making hasty judgments; and avoid triangulation by encouraging complainants to speak directly to those involved

- Foster understanding, forgiveness, and reconciliation, in cases where the rector, staff, or vestry is beleaguered or being overly criticized

- Ensure that policies and procedures are in place and enforced regarding employee or volunteer misconduct; immediately take any questions, concerns, and complaints to the rector and/or appropriate authorities

- Support the rector in taking action when employees or volunteers are charged with misconduct or inappropriate behavior

- Take action to intervene promptly (with others as appropriate) in the event that the rector is charged with misconduct, has problems with drugs or alcohol, or is acting inappropriately; speak with the rector and the bishop

- Petition the bishop in writing on behalf of the vestry to intervene in cases where conflict imperils the pastoral relationship between the rector and the congregation

- Encourage the rector to take corrective steps as appropriate in cases where the rector is overworked, disregarding his or her health and well-being or the health of the rector's family

- Assist in the identification of persons for leadership roles and participate in inviting them to serve in those roles

- Be prepared to assist the rector or to step in and do what is necessary (represent the congregation at community meetings, take responsibility for preparing the church for special events, advocate on behalf of the congregation, etc.)

- With the rector, announce the bishop's pending visit and prepare information on the spiritual and temporal state of the congregation to be discussed during his or her visit (Title III. Canon 9, Section 5b)

- When the congregation is without a rector:

    Notify the bishop promptly and make provisions for worship services (Title III. Canon 9, Section 6d)

    Lead the congregation by ensuring that:

    - The worship services, program, and pastoral care needs are being met

    - The selection process for a new rector has begun

    - Employee relations and communications with the diocese are maintained

- Ensure the name of the person proposed to be called as rector is submitted to the bishop thirty days before the election is to be held and deliver written notice of the election of a rector to the bishop (Title III. Canon 9, Section 3a (2&3))

- Prepare a Letter of Agreement with the proposed new rector, which outlines mutual responsibilities and is subject to the bishop's approval. Check with your diocese for sample letters. (Title III. Canon 9, Section 3a (4))

Additional responsibilities

The following responsibilities may not apply in all congregations. They are often more applicable in smaller congregations, especially those without full-time clergy. In cases where the clergy's role is limited to providing Sunday services and pastoral care, the wardens may provide the primary leadership in the congregation. In some congregations, tradition dictates the senior warden provide more leadership.

- Conduct the vestry meetings in the absence of, or when delegated by, a rector or priest-in-charge. While the canons designate the rector as the one to preside at vestry meetings, he or she may delegate this responsibility

- Conduct the annual meeting. Again, the rector often does this but in some congregations, the senior warden takes this responsibility

- Make the Sunday morning announcements

- Visit anyone known to have a major problem with a program, vestry decision, clergy, etc. in consultation with, and often accompanied by, the rector

Accountability

The senior warden is elected and accountable to the rector and the vestry. In some dioceses and congregations, the rector selects the senior warden.

- Adopt the practice of creating a covenant (promise) in which both the rector and the senior warden agree on the roles and responsibilities of the warden. This should be developed, and then reviewed annually, in a conversation with the vestry and in place before the election/selection of the senior warden.

- The senior warden's ministry should be considered as part of the annual mutual ministry review of the congregation.

Junior Warden Job Description

These are in addition to the requirements and responsibilities of all vestry members.

Time commitment

- Weekly meetings with the rector, if requested

Responsibilities

- Assist the rector and senior warden in providing leadership so the vestry can identify the mission, vision, and goals of the congregation; make and implement plans; assess programs; and celebrate achievements

- Provide leadership in the congregation by demonstrating a consistently positive attitude that seeks to resolve problems, recognizes accomplishments, and gives thanks for those things that build community and further the mission and vision of the church

- Work closely with the rector and senior warden in providing overall leadership of the congregation

In congregations where this position is responsible for property management and maintenance

- Have an understanding of property management and maintenance needs

- Have an ability to work with service people and to recruit and motivate members of the congregation to take responsibility for maintenance work

- Establish and execute a plan for and oversight of seasonal maintenance of all equipment (furnace, air conditioning, plumbing, kitchen facilities, office equipment, etc.)

- Establish and oversee a process for annual safety checks

- Review insurance needs with the treasurer and insurance agent; revise annually as needed

- Establish and oversee a process for obtaining the service of contractors as needed

- Chair or work with the head of a maintenance committee. If such a group exists, the above responsibilities may be delegated among the members with the warden providing primary oversight on behalf of the vestry

- Chair or work with an appointed group to oversee new building construction or renovation and property acquisition or disposal

- Consult with the vestry and rector on whether or not to accept gifts of real property to the parish

If the junior warden is not responsible for property matters, it is advisable to have a designated individual or committee charged with building and property management.

Other responsibilities

In congregations where the junior warden automatically succeeds the senior warden, learn the roles and responsibilities of the senior warden.

Accountability

- The junior warden is elected and accountable to the rector and the vestry.

- Adopt the practice of creating a covenant (promise) in which both the rector and the junior warden agree on the roles and responsibilities of the warden. This should be developed, and then reviewed annually, in a conversation with the vestry and in place before the election/selection of the junior warden.

- The junior warden's ministry should be considered as part of the annual mutual ministry review of the congregation.

Treasurer Job Description

These are in addition to the requirements and responsibilities of all vestry members.

Time commitment

- Weekly oversight of collections and deposits

- Periodic payment of bills

- Monthly generation of accounting reports

Responsibilities

- Supervise the collection, counting, and deposit of all contributions to the faith community, ensuring that at least two persons are present at all times during the collection and counting process

- Supervise the treasurers of all other accounts, ensuring that they follow established accounting procedures and appropriate safeguards (those accounts maintained by any organization/committee/task force that is part of the congregation)

- Ensure that bills are paid in a timely fashion

- Work with any designated committee to make certain that adequate insurance is maintained on all real property

- Determine that the books and accounts of the congregation are kept in accordance with standard accounting procedures and the requirements of the canons

- Ensure that the congregation's financial operations are in accordance with The Episcopal Church's and diocesan canons, congregational bylaws, and state and federal laws

- Ensure that the congregation's deeds and other instruments of ownership are secure and maintained in the manner prescribed by canon and civil law

- Ensure that anyone serving as custodian of any congregational or organizational funds over $500 is bonded by a professional bonding insurer

- Meet regularly with the rector, wardens, and/or staff for planning and evaluation

- Develop (if one does not exist) and serve on the finance committee

- Assist in the development of budgets

- Be available to consult with other committees that might need help in planning budgets or other assistance with financial matters

- Submit a monthly financial report to the vestry and an annual financial report to the congregation

- Make appropriate contributions to the diocesan parochial report

Accountability

- The treasurer may be elected or appointed as provided for by diocesan canon or congregational bylaws. The treasurer is accountable to the rector and vestry, and depending on the diocesan canon or congregational bylaws, may or may not be a member of the vestry.

- Adopt the practice of creating a covenant (promise) where the treasurer, rector, and the vestry agree on the roles and responsibilities of the treasurer. This should be developed, and then reviewed annually, in a conversation with the vestry and in place before the election/selection of the treasurer.

- The treasurer's ministry should be considered as part of the annual mutual ministry review of the congregation.

Secretary/Clerk Job Description

These are in addition to the requirements and responsibilities of all vestry members.

Time commitment

- Distribution of agenda and minutes from previous meetings

- Maintain roster of members and contact information

- Other duties as deemed necessary by the rector and senior warden

Responsibilities

- Take notes during vestry meetings and afterwards, prepare and distribute minutes

- Maintain a file of all vestry meeting minutes

- If asked, take minutes for the annual congregation meeting

- Prepare, date, sign, and maintain documents as required

Accountability

- The secretary/clerk may be elected or appointed as provided for by diocesan canon or congregational bylaws.

- The secretary/clerk is accountable to the rector and vestry.

- A covenant between the secretary/clerk, rector, and the vestry should be developed and reviewed annually.

- The secretary's/clerk's ministry should be considered a part of the annual mutual ministry review.

Additional sample vestry job descriptions are available on ECF Vital Practices (ecfvp.org/topics).

Recognizing that Holy Scripture will be our authority governing our behavior and relationships with one another and with the congregation, and acknowledging Saint Paul's directive to Timothy (*1 Timothy 4:12*) concerning his role as church leader to be "an example to the believers in speech, life, love, faith, and purity," we therefore agree to the following covenant.

To love one another by:

- Creating and nurturing within the vestry a safe and trusting atmosphere in which all members can feel comfortable and confident in expressing their thoughts and opinions

- Being sensitive to the different styles and personalities of individual vestry members

- Seeking to validate, appreciate, acknowledge, and understand the unique and special gifts of each vestry member

Treating each vestry member with respect by:

- Speaking and acting in such a way as to build up and support one another

- Confronting issues without demeaning anyone

- Refusing to listen to backbiting or gossip, especially about or from our church leaders

- Insisting that people who have accusations to make against another church leader do so in the presence of that individual

- Recognizing that certain discussions are of a confidential nature, thus maintaining good and wise judgment in respecting confidentiality

- Confronting with love those individuals who have hurt me in any way

- Following Saint Matthew's principle *(Matthew 18:15-17)* for conflict resolution between individuals: speaking first to the individual alone; if to no avail, bringing another (vestry member) into the conversation; and then, if necessary, finally referring the matter to the larger church (entire vestry)

- Practicing forgiveness for those I feel have wronged me

- Seeking to encourage those vestry members who may be suffering through trials of one kind or another

- Nurturing a servant attitude of serving both God and God's church

To seek God's will by striving for unity in all matters through:

- Joining the entire vestry in submitting significant matters to prayer, especially prior to voting or decision-making

- Upholding the final decision of the vestry even when I may disagree

- Always seeking to better understand others

- Submitting to one another in love

- Refraining from all discussions and conversations that are unwholesome and from a divisive course

- Consciously seeking to abandon personal agendas and self-serving attitudes

To be an example to the congregation by striving to:

- Faithfully attend sabbath worship

- Consistently engage in the study of Holy Scripture

- Live out the Christian life through regular, sacrificial giving, and making an annual pledge to support the ministry and mission of the church

- Support the church through active attendance and participation

- Be faithful to the (name of the church) mission and vision statement

Sample covenant based on document from St. Thomas Church in the Fields, Gibsonia, Pennsylvania, Episcopal Diocese of Pittsburgh.

Who Wouldn't Like a More Productive Meeting?

Monthly vestry meetings are too often testaments to endurance rather than efficiency. A three-hour meeting is rarely twice as productive as a ninety-minute meeting. And, each hour of a meeting consumes one hour of time for every person at the table. For a rector, vestry of twelve, and a treasurer, that three-hour meeting consumed forty-two hours—an entire individual work week.

The monthly meeting is the most valuable time the vestry expends, so it should yield the highest return. It should be used to do those things that you can only do, or best do, together. This requires minimizing the amount of passive participation during a meeting—time when everyone sits and listens to one person give an oral report, or when everyone reads a report or document passed out at the meeting and that, for some reason, everyone thinks needs to be dealt with tonight.

How do we trim time from our vestry meetings? In the Episcopal Diocese of Texas, we recommend vestries consider the practice of using a consent agenda for routine and procedural decisions.

What is a Consent Agenda?

A consent agenda is a collection of items that require action by the vestry but that can be dispatched without further discussion, debate, or information.

Minutes of the previous meeting are a good example. Rather than taking time to: ask for a motion to approve the minutes; note the presence of a second; ask if there are any additions/corrections/deletions to the minutes; ask for any further discussion; and then call the question, the minutes are approved in a single, non-debatable motion along with a host of other items.

For a consent agenda to work, it is important that all the reports and items on the agenda are identified in advance and materials sent to members in a timely manner, giving all members time to read the material before coming to the meeting. This requires that the draft minutes be circulated for review and correction within one week of a meeting. Members then have a week to submit corrections, additions, and deletions to the clerk or secretary, and the minutes are finalized and distributed at least one week prior to the next meeting where they are to be approved.

Another example is the rector's report. This should be written, but the rector should have time to briefly highlight or discuss sensitive matters orally during the meeting.

How Does the Consent Agenda Fit with the Meeting Agenda?

The consent agenda is one of the listed items in the business meeting agenda. Usually, it will fall in the first five items:

- Call to order and opening prayer
- Bible study or devotional
- Declaration of a quorum
- Adoption of the business meeting agenda
- Consent agenda
- (Balance of business meeting agenda)

How Does it Work?

The consent agenda lists each item, the action to be taken (received, approved) and the supporting detail for each item is attached to the consent agenda.

The consent agenda is moved, seconded, and voted on without discussion of any kind. This means everything on the agenda should be noncontroversial or already decided at a previous meeting. The motion is documented in the minutes and the consent agenda and all documentation is included with the minutes of the meeting in the official records of the congregation.

Any member may contact the chair *prior to the meeting* and request an item be removed due to a need for additional information, late-breaking developments, or further discussion. The item is struck from the agenda prior to the vote. It should not be moved to the business meeting agenda but rather handled "off line" or put on the agenda for the next meeting.

While each vestry is unique, a consent agenda should save thirty to sixty minutes per meeting. This opens up time for more strategic mission and ministry discussions and for shorter and more productive meetings.

Critical Success Factors

As a governance and strategic planning consultant, I need to spend at least two hours preparing for every hour I facilitate or consult. For a productive meeting, vestry members need to spend *at least* two hours preparing for each hour of the meeting. When this preparation is combined with the use of a consent agenda it can transform the members' productivity as well as their sense of accomplishment and satisfaction at the end of the meeting…and the meeting will be shorter.

This requires the business meeting agenda, consent agenda, and all supporting documents be in the hands of all members a minimum of one week prior to the meeting. Members who have questions should contact the appropriate individual prior to the meeting.

Sample Consent Agenda Items
Vestry Meeting – St. Swithen's Episcopal Church

- Approval of the minutes of the previous meeting
- Acceptance of reports: (specific action items come under new business)

  Committees of the vestry: (reports to the vestry, not copies of meeting minutes)

  Communications

  Evangelism

  Investment & Finance

  Outreach

  Strategic Planning

  Stewardship

  Junior Warden

  Rector

  Senior Warden

  Staff reports

- Affirming votes/decisions previously taken by electronic ballot (where canons and bylaws permit)
- Budget responsibility (designating staff or vestry with specific line item spending authority)
- Check signing authority (persons authorized to sign checks)
- Clergy housing allowance(s)
- Corporate resolutions (for banking or investment authority)
- Holiday schedule for coming year
- Committee or lay ministry appointments
- Policy and procedures
- Organization charts and job descriptions
- Committee charters

This Vestry Papers *article by Bob Schorr, manager of church plants and strategic development for the Episcopal Diocese of Texas, was published in January 2014 on the ECF Vital Practices website (ecfvp.org). It is reprinted with permission.*

How might you structure your vestry meeting to make time for missional leadership? The governance functions in this agenda are concentrated, allowing greater time for the development of an atmosphere of discipleship formation in the church so that the people will be equipped to serve the world in the name of Christ.

30 MINUTES

Gathering: Bible study and prayer. (For specific examples, see the resource section in *Cultivating the Missional Church: New Soil for Growing Vestries and Leaders* by Randolph Ferebee).

0 MINUTES

Minutes: "Approved" as distributed with corrections received at any time.

5–10 MINUTES

Financial Report: Use language accessible to all with an executive summary. Report should highlight key points and any actionable items. A norm to be honored is highly focused discussion; general financial positions may be discussed here or in Discipleship or Mission.

10–15 MINUTES

Discipleship: Programmatic activity of the parish that forms disciples. Includes worship, formation, fellowship, and generosity (stewardship). Receive and discuss any discipleship-related matters pending from previous meetings.

15–30 MINUTES

Mission: Actions that send the baptized into the world (discipleship/apostleship). Includes service, financial support, evangelism, and social justice. Receive and discuss any mission-related reports pending from previous meetings.

0–10 MINUTES

Other items needing vestry attention: This is the "catch-all" time of the meeting for anything that doesn't fit into the main categories.

30 MINUTES

Leadership School: Leadership development is the focus of this segment. Includes time for study and reflection. (For specific examples, see resource section in *Cultivating the Missional Church).*

1 MINUTE

Sending: Personal and corporate mission is primed by being sent into the world to be a blessing.

NOTES

If every element of this order of meeting went to the maximum suggested time, the meeting would take about two hours. Note this is a maximum time frame; ninety minutes is a more likely time frame. It may be helpful to appoint a process observer in the implementation of this schedule. The observer, a member of the vestry, simply pays attention to the flow of the meeting, verbally marks the passage of time, and reports on her or his process observations at the end of the meeting. Some vestries find it permanently helpful for the clerk to verbally note the time lapses. This time framework helps remove the possibility of micromanagement so that the vestry may concentrate on the big picture, the overall vitality of the church.

It is very likely that this Order of Meeting will need to be gradually implemented. The four key elements of Bible study, tending to discipleship, raising up apostles (mission activity), and the leadership school may be introduced in this way:

- Continue your present practice of opening devotions and prayer. Ask half the vestry to focus attention to discipleship formation within your normal meeting format; ask the other half to be attentive listeners for mission activity. Add the leadership school time at the end. Before entering the leadership school portion of the meeting, ask the listeners to report on what they heard through focused attention. This action begins to form the attention of members of the vestry. Note that many parts of a discussion may actually have both missional (or apostolic) and discipleship as components. Attention will likely be drawn to parts of parish life that reflect neither.

- All items brought before the vestry requiring action (except for emergencies) are placed on a thirty-day clock. This practice is that no action be taken on items introduced for the first time. Consequently, two gifts are given: there is no "tyranny of urgency" and time is amplified to ponder the step. This includes, for example, a finance report. Those who have ideas about what is presented at one vestry meeting can seek details in the intervening time and be prepared to accept the report (as is or modified) at the next meeting.

- When a decision is made, especially those that might be referred to as "actionable items," it is a good practice to append a simple list to the minutes of any open or not-yet-accomplished item. This list is visited regularly during the "other items" section of the meeting for purposes of accountability and tracking. These actionable items may also be considered, as appropriate, in the discipleship section or mission section. The key point here is that important decisions be provided support and follow-through.

- Consensus formation is the recommended model for decision-making. In an action that is pro forma, consensus may be noted simply by anyone saying, "I propose that the vestry accept this report by consensus." The chair then asks if there is consensus, "Is this the mind of the vestry?" Members of the vestry then give their assent (or not).

- Reports from members of the vestry or others who have worked for the good of the church's ministries and mission are always received gratefully and, if action is required, with a predisposition to say, "yes" to what is presented or requested. This is the nature of a permission-giving church; it seeks to offer creative space for the work of the Spirit in others. The vestry should inform all who are bringing reports or requests that require action before the vestry about the "thirty-day clock" on taking action.

An extension of being a permission-giving church is captured in the question, "Does it need to come before the vestry?" When a church is dedicated to the extension of the gospel of Jesus Christ, there will be many nudges from the Spirit that call the baptized into service. The vestry will find itself, when it is missional, more in the mode of simple gratitude and less in the mode of being.

Excerpted from Cultivating the Missional Church: New Soil for Growing Vestries and Leaders *by Randolph Ferebee and reprinted with permission, Church Publishing, 2013.*

VESTRY STEWARDSHIP STATEMENT: CREATING A CULTURE OF GIVING

John Lennon promoted the use of the imagination as a way to change the way people thought about the world, their place in it, and what it might take to change the world. He invited us to dream and hope and invite others into imagining what life could be.

Congregational life deserves the same gift of imagination. How might your congregation look if the gathered community grounded their sense of self-worth, accomplishment, and meaning in the way they practiced sharing their bounty? Is this idealism? A wild dream? Or a realistic goal toward which congregational leadership might strive?

Want to take on the challenge? One very important tool in such an endeavor is the crafting of a financial stewardship statement by the vestry. The purpose of the statement is twofold:

1. To give vestry members a vehicle to offer public reflection about how each experiences God in the midst of financial decision-making.

2. To serve as a basis for discussing financial leadership with prospective vestry members.

The decision to compose the statement is best preceded by developing a plan for how to use the statement. The process of developing the statement is highly beneficial to those who participate in its drafting. But the ultimate goal of the statement is to begin to change the culture of the congregation; therefore, a plan of action is equally important to the process of drafting the statement.

It is possible to draft the essence of a statement in two hours. The core of the process is forty-five minutes of Bible study and reflection that is carefully designed to bring the tenets of Christian faith to bear on the pervasive anxiety about money that characterizes our culture. One particularly helpful passage is Matthew 6:24-33.

- Give everyone a copy of the passage. Have someone read the passage aloud and ask everyone to listen for and underline the things that God is asking of us in the passage.

- Compile the answers in a column on the left side of an easel pad.

- Read the passage a second time and ask people to listen for and mark the things that God is promising us in the passage.

- Record the answers on a column on the right hand side of the easel pad.

- Lastly, pose the question: What are the barriers that keep us from responding to what God asks of us and from enjoying the promises?

- Record those answers in a center column, between the demands and promises.

- Reflect with the group on how Jesus comes to reconcile us to God and to help us respond in faithfulness and then enjoy the fullness of God's blessing.

Following the Bible study and reflection, divide the vestry into three small groups, each assigned to answer one of the following questions:

1. What do I believe about God and money? The statement begins with: WE BELIEVE…

2. What am I committed to doing about making my faith and my relationship with God a more integral part of how I think and act about financial decisions? The second paragraph begins with: WE COMMIT…

3. To what action, process, practice, and/or reflection do I want to invite the congregation? The last paragraph begins with: WE INVITE…

Give twenty to thirty minutes for the small groups to compose a statement that answers each of these questions. Have each group share their statement with the whole group and record the feedback. Then form a small group to take the feedback and the small group statements and craft a proposed draft of a complete statement. Present the draft for a period of reflection and feedback at a subsequent vestry meeting, and when ready, approve it.

The goal is not to get the strongest theological statement possible. The goal is to articulate a statement that everyone on the vestry can honestly endorse and reflect publicly on what it means in his or her own life.

The written statement can also take the form of a collect such as this one written by the vestry of Trinity Episcopal Church in Swanton, Vermont, as part of their annual commitment program:

> [We believe that] *God, who is the giver of every good gift, you are ever present in our lives and in the world. You act through us, your people, to care for and provide for everyone.*
>
> [We invite] *We pray for the courage to break out of our insecurity and fear around money as we deepen our understanding of our relationship to you and how we use our financial resources to do your work in the world.*
>
> [We commit] *We pray these things that we might know you better, that you will increase our desire and ability to give and help others through ministry and friendship and to gratefully commit ourselves to the work you have given us to do.* Amen.

Imagine. Just imagine what our faith communities might be and do if our notions of "success" were measured by our ability and capacity to give rather than accumulate, if we saw the world as place where we could share the abundance with which God has blessed us, if our experience of being blessed was grounded in our practice of generosity. Just imagine.

This ECF Vital Practices blog post by Angela Emerson, minister for stewardship development, The Episcopal Church in Vermont, originally appeared as an article in The Steward's Well, *an online publication of The Episcopal Church's Office of Stewardship. It is reprinted with permission.*